3m+

1200

Ernst Lehner

ALPHABETS & ORNAMENTS

DIVINO
AVXILIO

Alphabetum Flandricum.

Salomon Henrix scri.

DOVER PUBLICATIONS, INC.

New York

This Dover edition, first published in 1968, is an unabridged republication of the work originally published by The World Publishing Co., 1952. Several pages were printed in red and black ink in the original edition, and these plates are reproduced entirely in black in the present Dover edition.

Library of Congress Catalog Card Number: 68-19170

Manufactured in the United States of America
Dover Publications, Inc.
180 Varick Street
New York, N. Y. 10014

To Hansi

ACKNOWLEDGMENT

I WANT TO express my sincere gratitude and appreciation to my friends and colleagues, and to the librarians, collectors and book dealers in Europe and in the United States of America, who provided me over the years with suggestions, advice, information, research material and prints which led to the compilation of this book. Only their untiring help and encouragement made it possible.

Because they are too numerous to be thanked individually, I beg each one of them to accept this acknowledgment as my personal recognition of my indebtedness to him.

To Miss Ruth Goldberg of New York go my special thanks for her most helpful and friendly collaboration.

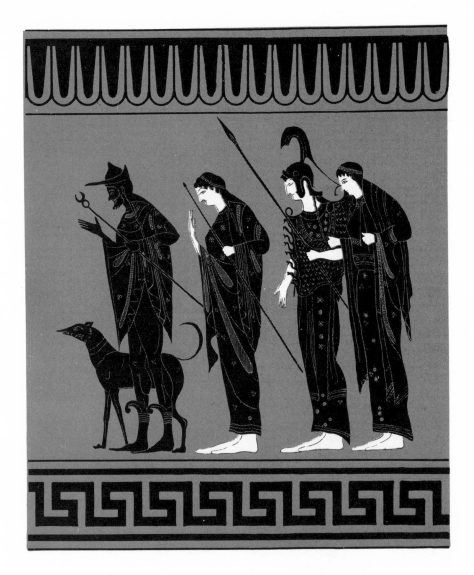

Silhouette painting from a Greek vase

LIST OF CONTENTS

Silhouette Painting   vi

Tattoo   xii

INTRODUCTION   xiii

TITLE PAGES AND FRONTISPIECES   15-56

The first ornamented title page printed by Erhard Ratdolt, Venice 1476   15
Index of illustrations   16-17
Text   18
The first book printed in North America by Stephen Day, Cambridge 1640   18
Ornamented title page printed by Erhard Ratdolt, Venice 1477   19
Ornamented Hebrew page printed by Elieser Toledano, Lisbon 1489   20
Title page printed by Conrad Dinckmut, Ulm 1493   21
Frontispiece printed by Pelegrino de Pasquali, Venice 1494   22
The first Serbo-Cyrillic title page by George Grnojević, Cetinje 1494   23
Frontispiece printed by Bernardinus Vercellensis, Venice 1495   24
The first German law book printed by Hans Schönsperger, Augsburg 1496   25
Ornamented title page printed at the Cistercian Monastery, Zinna 1496   26
Ornamented title page printed by Simon Papienses, Venice 1497   27
Ornamented title page printed by Johannes Winterburger, Vienna 1497   28
Frontispiece printed by Philippe Pigouchet, Paris 1498   29
Ornamented title page by Nicolo and Dominico Gesú, Venice 1500   30
Ornamented title page printed by Zorzi de Rusconi, Venice 1501   31
Title page printed by Johann Othmar, Augsburg 1502   32
Frontispiece printed by Stephanus Baland, Lyons 1505   33
Ornamented title page printed by Johannes de Rusconibus, Venice 1512   34
Title page designed by Daniel Hopfer, Augsburg 1515   35
Ornamented title page printed by Alessandro Paganino, Venice 1515   36
Ornamented title page from a Psalterium, Cologne 1518   37
Ornamented title page printed by Bernardinus de Vitalis, Venice 1521   38
Title page printed by Peter Treveris, London 1527   39
Hebrew title page printed by Gerson Cohen, Prague 1527   40
End page from the first mathematical book by Oronce Finé, Paris 1530   41
Title page designed by Hans Weiditz, Strasbourg 1530   42
Ornamented title page printed by Claude Nourry, Lyons 1532   43
Ornamented title page printed by Fridrich Peypus, Nuremberg 1532   44
Ornamented title page designed by Oronce Finé, Paris 1534   45
Title page printed by Rychard Grafton, London 1540   46
End page printed by Rychard Grafton, London 1548   47
Title page designed by Virgil Solis, Wittenberg 1558   48
Title page designed by Jost Amman, Frankfort o.M. 1570   49
Title page printed by Christoph Plantin, Antwerp 1578   50
Title page printed for Mathew Lownes, London 1605   51
Title page printed by Isaac Iaggard, London 1620   52
Title page designed by Jean-Michel Moreau the Younger, Paris 1769   53
Title page designed by William Morris, Kelmscott Press, Hammersmith 1892   54
Title page designed by Bertram G. Goodhue, De Vinne Press, New York 1893   55
Title page designed by Koloman Moser, Staatsdruckerei, Vienna 1904   56

LETTERS AND ALPHABETS   57-82

Initial from a manuscript, Toledo 11th century   57
Index of illustrations   58
Text   59
Initial from a manuscript, Germany 12th century   59
Ornamented Hebrew letters by Joshua Salomon Soncino, Cremona 1483   60
Ornamented alphabet, England 1490   61
Ornamented alphabet, Germany 15th century   61
Greek initials by Zacharias Callierges, Venice 1499   62-63

Initials from incunabula, Paris-Lyons 1485-1499   64-65
Children alphabet by Hans Weiditz, Augsburg 1521   66-67
Ribbon alphabet by Ludovico Vicentino, Venice 1533   68
Ornamented alphabet by Juan de Yciar, Saragossa 1550   68
Ornamented alphabet by Daniel Hopfer, Nuremberg 1549   69
Monograms and initials by Juan de Yciar, Saragossa 1550   69-71
Calligraphic initials by Amphiareo Vespasiano, Venice 1554   72
Alphabet by Giovanni Francesco Cresci, Rome 1569   73
Human alphabet by Jo.Theodor and Jo.Israel De Bry, Frankfort o.M. 1596   74
Ornamented alphabet, Italy 16th century   75
Initials by Lucas Kilian, Augsburg 1627   76-77
Initials by Johann Daniel Preisler, Nuremberg about 1700   78
Calligraphic alphabet by Mánoel Andrade de Figueiredo, Lisbon 1722   79
Ornamented alphabet, Austria 18th century   80
Wood and animal alphabets by Joseph Balthazar Silvestre, Paris 1843   81-82

FLEURONS AND BORDERS   83-106
The first "Fleurons" printed by Giovanni and Alberto Alvise, Verona 1478   83
Index of illustrations   84
Text   85
Typographic ornaments by William Caslon, Jr., London 1771   85
Typographic borders and ornaments by Georg Wolffger, Graz 1670   86-87
Typographic borders and ornaments by Louis René Luce, Paris 1740   88
Typographic anniversary broadside, Erfurt 1740   89
Title pages and ornaments by Pierre-Simon Fournier, Jr., Paris 1742-1766   90-91
Title page by Loyson & Briquet, Paris 1751   92
Title page by Johann Th. Trattner, Vienna 1760   92
Title page by Johannes Enschedé, Haarlem 1768   92
Typographic ornaments by Johann Thomas Trattner, Vienna 1760   93
Typographic colophons by C. & A. Adibert, Aix 1767-1773   94
Title page by Joseph Gillé, Paris 1773   95
Title page by Johann J. Engel, Pecs-Fünfkirchen 1773   95
Title page by Isaiah Thomas, Worcester, Mass. 1785   95
Typographic ornaments (First Empire), Paris 1810-1819   96
Typographic borders (Restauration), Paris 1820-1829   97
Border and ornaments by Andreäische Buchhandlung, Frankfort o.M. 1838   98-99
Typographic borders by A. Beyerhaus, Berlin 1840   100
Typographic borders (Louis Philippe), Paris 1840-1849   101
Typographic borders (Cathedral), Paris 1840-1849   102
Title page by John T. White, New York 1843   103
Typographic borders (Second Empire), Paris 1860-1869   104
Typographic border by Farmer, Little & Co., New York 1873   105
Typographic borders (Second Renaissance), Berlin 1870-1890   106

HEADPIECES AND VIGNETTES   107-122
Calligraphic endpiece from a manuscript, Paris 15th century   107
Index of illustrations   108
Text   109
Headpieces and vignettes by Aldus Manutius, Venice 1495-1499   109
Vignettes by Hans Holbein the Younger, London 1529   110
Headpieces by Ivan Fedorov, Moscow-Ostrog 1564-1580   111
Head- and endpieces, Paris 1630-1670   112-113
Headpieces by Vicentii Ursini, Naples 1681   114
Head- and endpieces by Johann Ernst Adelbulner, Nuremberg 1730   115
Head- and endpieces, Vienna 1740-1750   116
Head- and endpieces by Sigmund Calles, Vienna 1750-1760   117
Endpieces and vignettes by L'Imprimerie Royale, Paris 1760-1789   118
Head- and endpieces by L'Imprimerie Nationale, Paris 1792-1799   119
Vignettes by J. Ritchel von Hartenbach, Jr., Erfurt 1836   120-121
Vignettes by Aubrey Beardsley, Kelmscott Press, Hammersmith 1891-1895   122

SILHOUETTES AND SHADOW FIGURES 123-146
 Silhouette, India 123
 Index of illustrations 124
 Text 125
 Silhouettes, peasant art, Russia 125
 Shadow play pictures and figures, Siam 126-129
 Heads from shadow puppets, China 130-131
 Shadow puppets, Bali 132
 Intermission sign from a shadow play and shadow puppets, Java 133-135
 Shadow puppets, Turkey 136
 Shadow play figures, Mameluke, Egypt 14th century 137
 Lantern silhouettes, China 138-139
 Stencils for silk printing, Japan 140-141
 Silhouette "Calvary", Holland about 1700 142
 Silhouettes, peasant art, Italy 18th century 143
 Silhouettes, Vienna 18th century 144
 Silhouettes, monks art, Germany 19th century 145
 Silhouettes by Jean Jacob Hauswirth, Basel 1860 146

APPLIED ORNAMENTS AND PATTERN BOOKS 147-180
 Calligraphic ornament from a manuscript, England 12th century 147
 Index of illustrations 148
 Text 149
 Center pieces by Aldus Manutius, Venice 1499 149
 Needlepoint patterns by Albrecht Dürer, Nuremberg 1505 150-151
 Monstrances by Lucas Cranach, Wittenberg 1509 152-153
 Lace designs by Alessandro Paganino, Venice 1518 154-155
 Embroidery and lace designs by Nicolo Zoppino, Venice 1529 156-157
 Embroidery designs by Francisque Pellegrin, Paris 1530 158-159
 Embroidery designs by Peter Quentel, Cologne 1532 160-161
 Lace design by Giovanni Andrea Vavasore, Venice 1532 162
 Lace designs by Mattheo Pagan, Venice 1543 163
 Metal etching designs by Peter Flötner, Zurich 1546 164-165
 Embroidery designs by Giovanni Ostaus, Venice 1567 166
 Lace designs by Giacomo Franco, Venice 1596 167
 Lace designs by Hans Sibmacher, Nuremberg 1597 168-169
 Lace designs by Iaques Foillet, Montbeliard 1598 170-171
 Lace designs by Federic de Vinciolo, Paris 1606 172-173
 Designs for earrings, Holland 1609 174
 Wrought iron work designs by Hugues Brisville, Paris 1663 175
 Hilt and scabbard design by Antoine Jacquard, Poitiers 17th century 176
 Plaque designs by Henri Janssen, Amsterdam 17th century 177
 Curtain and panel designs by Daniel Marot, The Hague 1712 178-179
 Crochet type by L. Johnson & Co., Philadelphia 1873 180

SCRIPT AND SCROLLS 181-218
 Calligraphic colophon by Peter Schöffer, Paris 1449 181
 Index of illustrations 182-183
 Text 184
 Calligraphic letter, Germany 15th century 184
 Calligraphic book plates by Nicolas Flamel, Paris 14th century 185
 Ornamented title printed by M. P. Oliveri, Rouen 1490 186
 Calligraphic title printed by Wynkyn de Worde, London 1495 186
 Ornamented title page designed by Jean Duvet, Lyons 1496 187
 Calligraphic title printed by Anton Koberger, Nuremberg 1498 188
 Calligraphic title printed by Iaccuinus de Tridino, Venice 1502 188
 Ornamented title printed by Richard Pynson, London 1515 189
 Calligraphic title printed by Johannes Taccuinus, Venice 1517 189
 Calligraphic title by Melchior Lotter, Wittenberg 1522 190
 Calligraphic page by Nicolaus Werner, Germany 16th century 190
 Ornamented pages by Giovanni Antonio Tagliente, Venice 1524 191

Title page printed by Mathias Apiarius, Bern 1539   192
Title page printed by Christoph Froschauer, Zurich 1548   193
Title page, frontispiece and lettering by Caspar Neff, Cologne 1549   194-195
Calligraphic broadside, Nuremberg 1571   196
Title page by Jacob Jacobelln, Strasbourg 1579   197
Ornamented page from a manuscript, Germany 16th century   197
Calligraphic pages by Jan van den Velde, Rotterdam 1605   198
Calligraphic page by De Beaugrand, Paris 1601   199
Calligraphic title page by Maria Strick, Delft 1607   199
Ornamented pages by Salomon Henrix and Petrus Bales, Amsterdam 1614   200
Calligraphic title page by Richard Gething, London 1619   201
Calligraphic page by Perriccioli, Siena 1619   201
Scrolls by Geobattista Pisani, Genoa 1640   202
Scrolls by Edward Cocker, London 1657-1672   203-204
Scrolls by John Seddon, London 1695   205
Calligraphic merchants' diploma, Leipzig 1699   206
Calligraphic page by John Clark, London 1714   206
Ornamented pages by Michael Baurenfeind, Nuremberg 1716   207
Scrolls by Mánoel Andrade de Figueiredo, Lisbon 1722   208-209
Ornamented page by Johann Georg Schwandner, Vienna 1756   210
Ornamented pages by Johann Merken, Mühlheim 1782   211
Scroll by Joaquim José Ventura da Silva, Lisbon 1803   212
Scroll by Johann Evangelist Mettenleiter, Munich 1850   212
Hebrew title from a manuscript, Germany 10th century   213
Hebrew title from a manuscript, Cologne 1571   213
Kufic-Arabic leaf from the Koran, Mesopotamia 7th century   214
Kufic-Arabic leaf from the Koran, Mesopotamia 9th century   214
Arabic leaf from the Koran, North Africa 15th century   215
Calligraphic proverb (Bismillah), Persia 17th century   215
Calligraphic signature (Bismillah) of Emir Beha Ullah, Persia   216
Signature (Thugra) of Sulaiman I the Magnificent, Turkey 1520-1566   216
Rosace from the mosque of Sulaiman I, Constantinople 16th century   217
Arabic inscription from the Alhambra, Granada 13th century   217
Calligraphic inscription by Emperor T'ai-Tsung, China 970-998   218

HERALDIC ORNAMENTS AND ALLEGORIC CARTOUCHES   219-246

Seal of Edward the Confessor, England 1043-1066   219
Index of illustrations   220-221
Calligraphic sigil of Alfonso the Wise, Spain 1226-1284   221
Text   222
Seal of Rudolf I of Hapsburg, Holy Roman Emperor, 1273-1291   222
Seal of Margaret of France, 1299   223
Seal of Thomas De Beauchamp, 1369   223
Seal of John Holland, 1436   223
Seal of Robert De Hungerford, 1449   223
Tree of affinity printed by Ludwig Hohenwang, Augsburg 1477   224
Tree of affinity printed by Joannes Hamman de Landoia, Venice 1490   224
Pedigree of Leapold zu Babenberg, Basel 1491   225
Family diagram of Albrecht von Sachsen, Mainz 1492   226
Tree of succession, Basel 1499   226
Tree of succession, France 15th century   226
Heraldic title page printed by Thielmann Kerver, Paris 1500   227
Religious diagrams by Jacob de Leucho, Venice 1504   228
Religious diagram by Gotardo da Ponte, Venice 1510   228
Heraldic title page printed by Diego de Gumiel, Valencia 1515   229
Heraldic title page by Casper Clofigl, Munich 1518   230
Emperor Maxmilian I by Albrecht Dürer, Nuremberg 1519   231
Pedigree of Maxmilian I by Albrecht Dürer, Nuremberg 1515-1519   232-233
The great seal and counter seal, England 1527   234
Cartouches by Donato Aelio, Venice 1532   234

Family tree of Ferdinand of Austria by Robert Peril, Amsterdam 1540   235
Cartouche "Saint Sebaldus", Nuremberg 1540   235
Map cartouche by Lafreri, Rome 1546   236
Religious diagram by Hugo à Porta, Lyons 1559   236
Allegoric title page printed by Lorenzo Torrentino, Florence 1551   237
Heraldic title page, Ingolstadt 1553   238
Allegoric title page by Matheus Merian, Basel 1555   239
Map cartouches by Abraham Ortelius, Antwerp 1570-1584   240
Pedigree of King Henry VIII, London 1561   241
Cartouches by F. de Wit, Antwerp 1568   242
Sigil of the University of Oxford, 16th century   242
Seal and counter seal of the Kings Council, Colony of Virginia 1606   242
Book stamp of Jacopo Bocampagni, Duke of Sora, 1612   243
Book stamp of John Williams, Bishop of Lincoln, 1642-1650   243
Sigil of Governor Peter Stuyvesant, New Netherland 1647-1664   243
The great seal of King William III and Queen Mary, England 1689-1695   243
Map cartouches, Italy 17th century   244
Sigil of the Printers Guild, Jena 1720   245
Diagram of the Printers Guild, Regensburg 1740   245
Book stamp of Baptist Noel, Earl of Gainsborough, 1714   246
Book stamp of Hugh Boscawen, Viscount Falmouth, 1715   246
Book stamp of Pope Pius VI, Rome 1775-1799   246

BIBLIOGRAPHY   247-256
The K. K. Garellian Public Library, Vienna 1780   247

Endpiece/GERMANY 1880

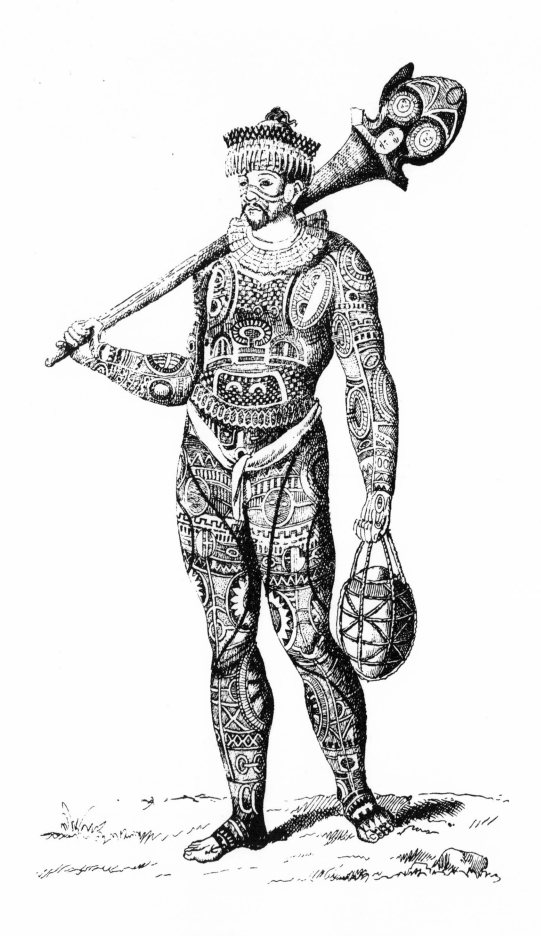

Tattoo of a Nukahiva priest, Marquesas Islands

INTRODUCTION

THE LUST to decorate and to embellish is part and parcel of the creative impulses of man. Somehow plain surfaces and clear outlines attract and intrigue the human eye, and man always endeavors to improve and beautify these challenging spaces and lines neglected by nature. This desire of man to ornament is not bound to any era, continent, race, cultural or educational standard. It has subconscious roots in every human being. We can observe it in the irresistible urge of small children everywhere to "decorate" any plain space or empty wall within their reach, and in the absent-minded doodling of grownups on pads and papers.

We can follow this urge to decorate from the dawn of human history right through all the ages and civilizations. From the plain wall sketches of the cave dwellers to the elaborate murals of our ocean liners. From the simple scratch designs on some of the crude implements of the Stone, Copper and Iron Ages to our own sophisticated and ornate table wares and household objects. From the little known art of decorative tattoo (developed from primitive scars of prehistoric times and still practiced by some African and Oceanian tribes) to the highly artistic ornaments of symbolic body decoration of Polynesia. From the war paint and battle finery of savage warriors to heraldic regalia and our military distinctions. From coarse grass and fiber tissues embellished with seashells, feathers and nutshells to beautifully ornamented fabrics, embroideries and laces.

Our information on ornamental art of early times is indirect and spotty, pieced together from some fragments of architectural designs, stone carvings and other archeologic odds and ends. Unfortunately man's work is as brittle and destructible as man himself. It is prey not only to the consuming forces of the elements of nature but also to the destructive furor of his fellow-man in wars and upheavals.

Our knowledge of decorative forms and expressions in antiquity is a little more intimate, thanks to the plentiful discoveries of archeologists at the sites of vanished cultures in Egypt, Nubia, Babylonia, Assyria, Phoenicia, Greece, Etruria, Rome, Persia, Media, India, the Far East, Central and South America. Wall carvings, tile pavements, mosaic incrustations, vase paintings, household objects, arms, and jewelry found in tombs, temples and other ruins give us a more than fleeting glance at the enormous development of applied art in these cultural periods.

We have gained a fair knowledge of ornamental art from the beginning of the Christian and Byzantine era throughout the Dark Ages, from paintings on wood panels, illuminated manuscripts and an impressive array of similar sources. Thorough and complete information on all these periods can be gained by the student of applied art from the many elaborate and excellent books on these special subjects by outstanding historians and scholars. The invention of paper in Europe in the fourteenth century, and of printing in the fifteenth century enabled our European forefathers to hand down to us a broad and complete picture of their decorative and ornamental designs in everyday use.

Artists, designers, craftsmen, printers, typographers, art students and amateurs who are seeking inspiration and a more intimate acquaintance with the decorative art of this period must spend a lot of time searching for manuscripts and incunabula, rare books and atlases, design and pattern books of the old masters and craftsmen. Even contemporary books on these subjects, published only a few decades ago, already belong to the rare book class. It takes a good portion of bibliographic know-how to look for and to locate such rare volumes. They are mostly found in separate rare book departments of universities, museums, private and public libraries. These special collections are sometimes not accessible to the average reader, but only to the scholar, the bibliophile and the researcher.

The material reproduced in this book was selected and compiled by the author with one thought in mind: to give the reader the possibility of visualizing in chronological order the fantastic abundance of designs in some of the main groups of applied ornaments and decorations of the last five hundred years, without the necessity and strain of plowing through acres and acres of books and prints.

For the benefit of the interested student and amateur of applied art, an extensive bibliography on many subjects of decoration and ornament has been included in this book.

Q Vesta opra da ogni patte e un libro doro
Non fu piu preciosa gemma mai
Dil kalendario : che tratta cose asai
Con gran facilita : ma gran lauoro
Qui numero aureo : e tutti i segni fuoro
Descripti dil gran polo da ogni lai :
Quando ti sole : e luna eclipsi fai :
Quante terre se rece a sto thexoro.
In un instanti tu sai qual hora sia :
Qual sara lanno ; giorno : tempo : e mexe :
Che tutti ponti son dastrologia .
Ioanne de monte regio questo fexe :
Coglier tal frutto acio non graue sia
In breue tempo : e con pochi penexe .
Chi teme cotal spexe
Scampa uirtu. I nomi di impressori
Son qui da basso di rossi colori .

Venetijs. 1476

Bernardus pictor de Augusta
Petrus loslein de Langencen
Erhardus ratdolt de Augusta

The first ornamented title page printed by Erhard Ratdolt / VENICE 1476

TITLE PAGES AND FRONTISPIECES

PAGE 15

The first ornamented title page from Johannes Monteregio's "Calendarium", printed by Erhard Ratdolt, Venice 1476.

PAGE 18

Title page from "The Whole Booke of Psalmes", the first book printed in North America by Stephen Day, Cambridge, Mass. 1640.

PAGE 19

Ornamented title page from "Appiani Alexandrini Romanorum Historiarum", printed by Erhard Ratdolt, Venice 1477.

PAGE 20

Ornamented Hebrew page from David ben Josef Abuderahim's "Commentarius super ordinem precum", printed by Rabbi Elieser Toledano, Lisbon 1489.

PAGE 21

Title page from Bertoldus' "Das andächtig zeytglöcklein des lebes un leydens Christi", printed by Conrad Dinckmut, Ulm 1493.

PAGE 22

Frontispiece from Leonardo Bruni Aretino's "Opera intitolata l'Aquila", printed by Pelegrino de Pasquali, Venice 1494.

PAGE 23

The first Serbo-Cyrillic title page from "Octoëchos", printed by George Grnojević, Cetinje 1494.

PAGE 24

Frontispiece from Johann Antonio Campani's "Opera", printed by Bernardinus Vercellensis, Venice 1495.

PAGE 25

Frontispiece from Eike von Repkow's "Sachsen-spiegel", the first German law book, printed by Hans Schönsperger, Augsburg 1496.

PAGE 26

Ornamented title page from Hermann Nitschewitz's "Novum Beate Mariae Virgins Psalterium", printed at the Cistercian Monastery, Zinna 1496.

PAGE 27

Ornamented title page from "Iulii Firmici Materni de Nativitatibus", printed by Simon Papienses dictus Bevilaqua, Venice 1497.

PAGE 28

Ornamented title page from "Practica auf dis iar MCCCCXCVII", printed by Johannes Winterburger, Vienna 1497.

PAGE 29

Ornamented frontispiece from Simon Vostre's "Livre d'Heures", printed by Philippe Pigouchet, Paris 1498.

PAGE 30

Ornamented title page from "Vita di sancti padre", printed by Nicolo and Dominico Gesú, Venice 1500.

PAGE 31

Ornamented title page from Albertutio Vesputio Fiorentino's "Novo Mondo con veduta di Venezia", printed by Zorzi de Rusconi, Venice 1501.

PAGE 32

Title page from "Pomerium de Tempore", printed by Johann Othmar, Augsburg 1502.

PAGE 33

Frontispiece from "Missale ad usum romane eccelie", printed by Stephanus Baland, Lyons 1505.

PAGE 34

Ornamented title page from "M. Fabii Quintiliani Oratoriae Institutiones", printed by Johannes de Rusconibus, Venice 1512.

PAGE 35

Title page from "Chronicon Abbatis Urspergensis", designed by Daniel Hopfer, printed by Johann Miller, Augsburg 1515.

PAGE 36

Ornamented title page from "Apocalipsis iesu christi", printed by Alessandro Paganino, Venice 1515.

PAGE 37

Ornamented title page from "Psalterium in quatuor linguis", printed in Cologne 1518.

PAGE 38

Ornamented title page from "Publii Francisci Modesti Ariminensis", printed by Bernardinus de Vitalis, Venice 1521.

PAGE 39

Title page from "Polychronicon", printed by Peter Treveris, London 1527.

PAGE 40

Hebrew title page from Gerson Cohen's "Haggadah", Prague 1527.

PAGE 41
End page from the first mathematical book "Opus Varium", designed by Oronce Finé, Paris 1530.

PAGE 42
Title page from Oth. Brunfels' "Herbarum", designed by Hans Weiditz, printed by Johannes Schott, Strasbourg 1530.

PAGE 43
Ornamented title page from François Rabelais' "Pantagruel", printed by Claude Nourry, Lyons 1532.

PAGE 44
Ornamented title page from Martin Luther's "Der CXLVII Psalm Lauda Jerusalem", printed by Fridrich Peypus, Nuremberg 1532.

PAGE 45
Ornamented title page from "Orontii Finei Delphinatis Regii Mathematicarum Professoris", printed by Simon de Colines, Paris 1534.

PAGE 46
Title page from Cranmer's "The Byble in Englishe", printed by Rychard Grafton, London 1540.

PAGE 47
End page from Edwarde Halle's "Chronicle", printed by Rychard Grafton, London 1548.

PAGE 48
Title page from Martin Luther's "Biblia", designed by Virgil Solis, Wittenberg 1558.

PAGE 49
Title page from "In Studiosorum Gratiam", designed by Jost Amman, printed by Sigmund Feyerabend, Frankfort o.M. 1570.

PAGE 50
Title page from C. Sueton's "Vitae XII Caesarum", printed by Christoph Plantin, Antwerp 1578.

PAGE 51
Title page from Sir Philip Sidney's "The Countesse of Pembrokes Arcadia", printed for Mathew Lownes, London 1605.

PAGE 52
Title page from Giovanni Boccaccio's "The Decameron", printed by Isaac Iaggard, London 1620.

PAGE 53
Title page from "Les Graces", designed by Jean-Michel Moreau the Younger, printed for Laurent Prault, Paris 1769.

PAGE 54
Ornamented title page from Raoul Le Fleure's "The recuyell of the historyes of Troye", designed by William Morris, printed by Kelmscott Press, Hammersmith 1892.

PAGE 55
Ornamented title page from "The Book of Common Prayer", designed by Bertram Grovenor Goodhue, printed by De Vinne Press, New York 1893.

PAGE 56
Ornamented title page from "Zur Feier des Einhundertjährigen Bestandes der K. K. Hof- und Staatsdruckerei", designed by Koloman Moser, Vienna 1904.

TITLE PAGES AND FRONTISPIECES

IN THE first twenty years of printing with movable type, books contained no title pages. Their low price as compared with the cost of handwritten manuscripts, and their novelty value, gave these volumes enough sales attraction. The outer appearance of a book was not the printer-publisher's concern. Books were bound individually according to the collector's or librarian's taste and solvency.

In these two short decades, the skill of printing spread like wildfire over Europe. In the year 1476, over one hundred offices printed books. They were being printed all the way from Naples to London, from Lyons to Cracow, from Saragossa to Rostock. Competition became really keen. In that year, Erhard Ratdolt of Venice designed the first ornamented title page, to give his *Calendarium* a more eye-appealing appearance. Such decorated title pages and frontispieces immediately became a necessary feature for every book. Throughout the following centuries these decorative title pages and frontispieces were designed by the most outstanding artists of their time.

In the last century the invention of new printing processes brought on much larger editions of books. Their appearance and bindings became the concern of the publishers. The make-up of the bindings was highly embossed and brightly gilded while decorative and ornamented title pages declined in popularity.

The thorough commercialization of book production in our century went one step further. The bindings became more or less uniform. The decorative sales appeal, completely detached from the book, took on the form of the book jacket.

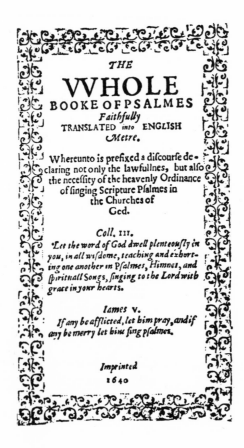

The first book printed in North America by Stephen Day / CAMBRIDGE 1640

Ad diuum Alfonfum Aragonum & utriufcp Sicilię
regem in libros ciuiliū bellorū ex Appinno Alexan-
drino in latinū traductos Pręfatio incipit feliciffime.

Arthorū regem ut ab Anneo accepi-
mus fine munere falurare nemo po-
teft. Ego uero gloriofiffime rex cum
tuam uirtutē bumanitatēcp cōfidero
cum ceteras naturę dotes: quibus in-
tet ętatis noftrę principes uel in pri-
mis illuftris es: fublime ingenium :
fummā caritatē: fummā continentiā
nulla ratione adduci poffum ut non
pluris apud te fidem meā effe exiftimem q̄ ullas opes. Quip-
pe cū te indigentibus & ueluti e naufragio emerfis q̄q̄ ignotis
offerre uideam pias manus. Cęteꝝ nec fine munere ad te ueni
nec uacuis(ut aiunt) manibus tuā maieftatē fum adoraturus .
Nam cū priotes Appiani libros, Libycum: Syrium: Partbicū
& Mitbridaticū Nicolao quinto fūmo pontifici dum i buma-
nis ageret e greco ttanftuliffem, Reliquos ciuilium bellorum
cōmentarios: quę Senatus: pupulucp romanus inuicem geffit
nundū editos aut perfectos a me ad quem potius mitterem q̄
ad te iuictiiffime princeps, Hifpanię pariter & Italię noftrę de-

Anneus Seneca de
rege parcborum.

Nicolaus papa quin-
Libycus.   (tus.
Syrius.
Parthicus.
Mitbridaticus.

Appiani Alexandrini fopbifte Romanorū liber finit
qui Celticus infcribatur.   Traductio. P. Candidi.

Impreffum eft boc opus Venetijs per Bernardū picto-
rem & Erbardum ratdolt de Augufta una cum Petro
loflein de Langencen correctore ac focio. Laus Deo.
.M. CCCC. LXXVII.

Ornamented title page printed by Erhard Ratdolt / VENICE 1477

עזר אלהי קדם שוכן
מעונה: אהל לפרש
תפלות כל השנה ::

אמן דוד בר יקף סע בר דוד מ בן חבוריס · ברוך יי לו אתא אברקס אשר
ביחר ם וכורטו אחריו עד עולם · נגב מטמט מעשף ידו שלם · זיקרבם לפב
קר סיט יקחאגד · וסאמישט תרדת נחאות מעמד · ויסב במשת רבת לתעלתי
לבגיל וכתש ותפאחרש · ישכן כסבו בתך עמו · נבת אשר ביחד לשימו
וקיס כל אים אשר נמצא את · שן אשר חטא או הרקוד במחשבת · מעא
חטיאת לבפר על חטיאת · או שלם על רות טונת · ושס אשוס אסם מעא על
אשמת · וכטת הקקרים קרבם ימתדיס פשרו רשעת · ועתיס יתרדק לפנ יון
בגרבם אשר נדבק רוחו · אות · ובהימלת יי על ענת · סת לקקריבבל יוס
ויס מזוקת · תמיד בשחר ותמיד מערב כהלבת · ובשטתת וברחשי תדשיס–
ובמועדיס · סת לקקריבכמו ספ על התמינים · וכולם יעלו לרסן למהכפר נהס
ירייס · ואחת קטבטרת אשר נתן תמילך לעהודיס · ושתח מפט חטיאים · חרב
סת קדסם ותפ צרחתם · ונגאש מיחרכם · ובטל קרבמתם · ואין אם יכולן לצעלת
עלותים כמטתם · תעמריס סדרן · ויוסטם כהלבתן · ואין חטיאת ואין אסס
ואין שלם · ואין עטביס מנכפרת על קקל קבולה · עד אשר כל אים מיאנסי
כנסת הגדולה חקך ודרס · ומצאו בספר תורת קטליס מעטרם · וצבדתם את לו
טיס · וטור ולמגדו בכל לבנטם · ואימרו חי זו קיא עטדיק סבלגב וו תפלם
תקן לו בחזבק וחמלה · לאותם לרסן בחרן עמיט · שבאלמה מריס סתתם ·
בכל יוס שלשת תפלות מסורדיס שתיס סבגד סת תמידיס קמכריס · וחית סבגד

Title page printed by Conrad Dinckmut / ULM 1493

Frontispiece printed by Pelegrino de Pasquali/VENICE 1494

ѠНЕ́ЖЕ ВЪ ТРОЙЦИ ПОКЛАНІА́ЕМІН
ЕГЬ БЛГОИЗВОЛН ИСПЛЪ́НИТИ СВО
ΙѠ ЦРКВЬ, РАЗЛИ́ЧНЫМИ КНИГА́МИ
ВИ ДѢ ВЬ А́ЗЬ ВЬ ХА́ БГА БЛГО В ТРН
ЫН И БМЬ ХРАНИ́МИ ГНЬ ГЮ́РГЬ ЦЬ
РНОЕ́ВИКЬ • ЦРКВЫ ПРАЗ ДНЫ СТЫ ХЬ
КНИГЬ, ГРѢ ХЬ РА́ДИ НАШИ ХЬ РАЗХН
ЩЕНІЕ́МЬ И РАЗ ДРАНІЕ́МЬ АГАРА́НСКЫ ХЬ ЧЕ́ДЬ • СЬ ЗРѢ
ВНОВА ХЬ ПОСПѢ́ШЕНІЕ́МЬ СТГО ДХА́ , И ЛЮ́БОВІЮ КЬ ЖЕ
ТВНЫМ ЦРКВАМ • И НАПИСАХЬ СІЮ ДШЕ́ПСНУЮ КНИ́ГУ Ѡ́С
МОГЛА́СНЫКЬ • ВЪ И́СПЛЪ́НИНІЕ СЛАВОСЛО́ВІЮ ТРИ́СЛНЧНА́Г
ОВЬ Е́ДИНСТВѢ ПОКЛАНІА́ЕМА́ГО БЖ́СТВА • МЛА́ЮЖЕ ЮНІЕ
И СЬВЗРА́СТНЫЕ И СТАРІЕ , ЧЬ ТО́УЩЕ́Н И ЛИ ВЬ СПѢ́ВАЮЩЕЙ
И ЛИ ПИ́ШУЩЕ ЛЮ́БВЕ ХВѢ РА́ДИ НИСПРАВЛІА́ТН • НА́С ЖЕ ОУ́СЬ
РДНЕ ПО ТЪ́ ЩАВШИ ХЬ СЕ НА СІЕ ДѢ́ЛО БЛ́СВЛІА́ТИ • ДА́ Ѡ́ БОИ
СЛА́ВѢ ЦІЕ Ѡ́ЦА И ЗНА ЕГО́ ЖЕ ВЬ СІА́ СНА И́ МЬ ЖЕ ВЬ СІА́ , СТГО ДХА́
Ѡ́ НІ́ ЕМ́ ЖЕ ВЬ СІА́ ЗДѢ Ѹ ОУ́ ЛУ́ЧИМ МИ́ЛАСТЬ ТА́МО ЖЕ СІН СВѢ
ТОМ Ѡ́ ЗА́РЫМ СЕ , А́МІН. ПОВЕЛѢ́НІЕМ ГНА́ МИ ГЮ́РГИА
ЦЬРНОЕ́ВИКИ А́ЗЬ ХУ́ДА́ БЬ СТЕ́НОИН ОКЬ МАКА́РІЕ , РОУ́КО
ДѢ́ЛИ САХ СІЄ̀. ПРИ ВСЕ Ѡ́ СЩЕ́ННОМ МИТ РО́ПОЛИТЕ ЗЕ́ТС
КОМ КУ́Р ВАВУ́ЛЕ • ВЬ ЛѢ́ТО · ЗА́ КРГ СЛНЦ, А̃ · ЛУНЕ, Ѳ̃ :·

The first Serbo-Cyrillic title page by George Grnojević / CETINJE 1494

Frontispiece printed by Bernardinus Vercellensis / VENICE 1495

The first German law book printed by Hans Schönsperger / AUGSBURG 1496

Actum hoc nonū et infrascri
ptum beate Marie virginis
psalteriū ad honoré onūpote
tis dei ad eusdē beate Marie
virginis celestis et terrestris
glose Jmpatricis Illustrissi
mi friderici tcij Jmpatoris
τ maximi Maximiliani glori
osissimi nostri regis ab earun
dem Illustrissimaτ regiaruτ
maiestatū buillimo Cappella
no Hermāno Mitzschewitz
er Brandeburgēsi Margia
Trebbinensi vtrinsqτ Jnris psul tu magno Cir
ca Oderam franckfordensis ciuitatis prothono
tario ad teucroτ cōtentōτ denoue legis dulcissi
mis mirabilibʒ diuini amoris flore vberrie referi
tis pfectū Annodomini Millesimoquadringē
tesimooctuogesimo Mono Illustrissimo Jmpa
tori friderico ex Lunenborch delatū Et Anno
Monagesimosecūdo in mense Septēbri ad Il
lustrissimas cesarias regiasqτ manʒ pficialit pre
sentati Mutti regio cesario iussu Ab illustrissi
ma Romana Friderici Jmpatoris tercij Can
cellaria examinatū Cesareo sumptu ad imprē
dum pmissum Msic et in Tzenna Cisterciensis
ordis deuoto claustro subpncipatu domni. dni
Micolai abbatis spiritualis patris ac domni dō
m sui graciosi singularissi in huius glose vginis
laudibʒ sui et tociʒ Cistersiensis ordinis dulcis
sime patronisse deuoti ad alti celsi sacri diui pij

Ornamented title page printed at the Cistercian Monastery / ZINNA 1496

CVM GRATIA ET
PRIVILEGIO.

¶Iulii Firmici Materni Iunioris Siculi Viri Clarissimi ad
Mauortiū Lollianum Fascibus Cápaniæ Romanæ prouin
ciæ procōsulem designatum ; per Diuum Cæsarem Consta
tinum Maximū Parrociniū defensionis Matheseos incipit.

PROOEMIVM.

LIM tibi hos libellos Mauorti
decus nostrum: editurg me esse
promiserā. Verg me diu incon
stātia uerecunde retardauit: &
ab isto scribendi studio dubia
trepidatio mie reuocauit. Cum
fragilitas ingenii mei nihil se
scire tale posse conciperet: qd
dignum fore tuis auribus iudi
caret Nam cum esses in cam-
paniæ prouinciæ fascibus costitutus: cuius te administratio
nis meritum maxima honoris dignitate nobilitat : occurri
tibi rigore hyemalium pruinarum: & prolixi itineris diuersi
tate confectus: illic tu languentis & fatigati corporis mei se
nium enixus es: & fidis: & religiosissimis amicitiæ releuare
fomentis. Cum itaçb ad pristinum statum me solatiis ac me
delis tuis sanitas restituta reuocasset : recolentes inuicem pri
stinos actus: & ad memoriam reuocantes: honestas & uari-
as sermonum fabulas serebamus. Posteaģ de talibus ac de p
cessibus nostris confabulati sumus: scrutatus mie es(sicut me
ministi)totius Siciliæ sicum: quam incolo: & unde oriun

Ornamented title page printed by Simon Papienses / VENICE 1497

Ornamented title page printed by Johannes Winterburger / VIENNA 1497

Frontispiece printed by Philippe Pigouchet / PARIS 1498

Ornamented title page by Nicolo and Dominico Gesú / VENICE 1500

Ornamented title page printed by Zorzi de Rusconi / VENICE 1501

Title page printed by Johann Othmar / AUGSBURG 1502

*Frontispiece printed by Stephanus Baland/*LYONS 1505

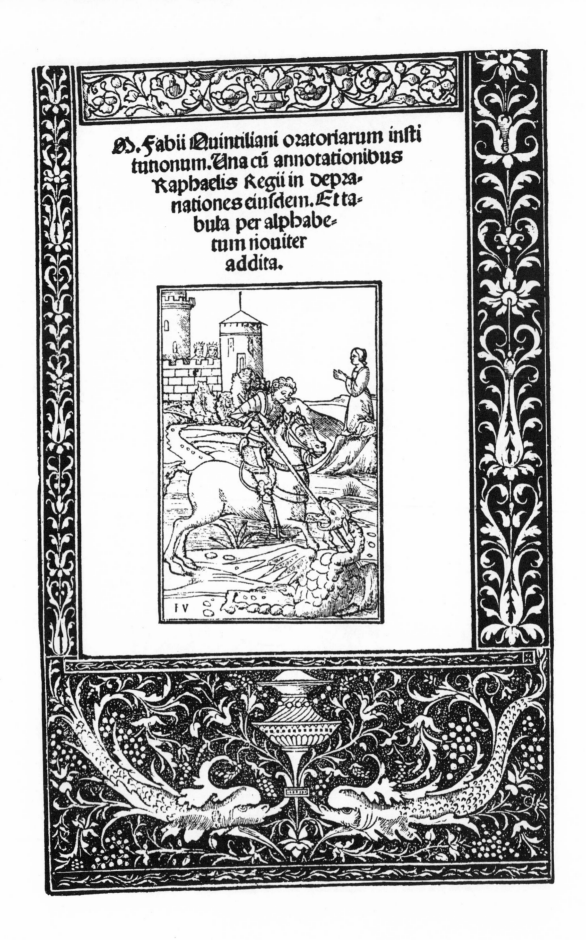

M. Fabii Quintiliani oratoriarum insti
tutionum. Una cũ annotationibus
Raphaelis Regii in depra=
nationes eiusdem. Et ta=
bula per alphabe=
tum nouiter
addita.

IV

Ornamented title page printed by Johannes de Rusconibus / VENICE 1512

Title page designed by Daniel Hopfer/AUGSBURG 1515

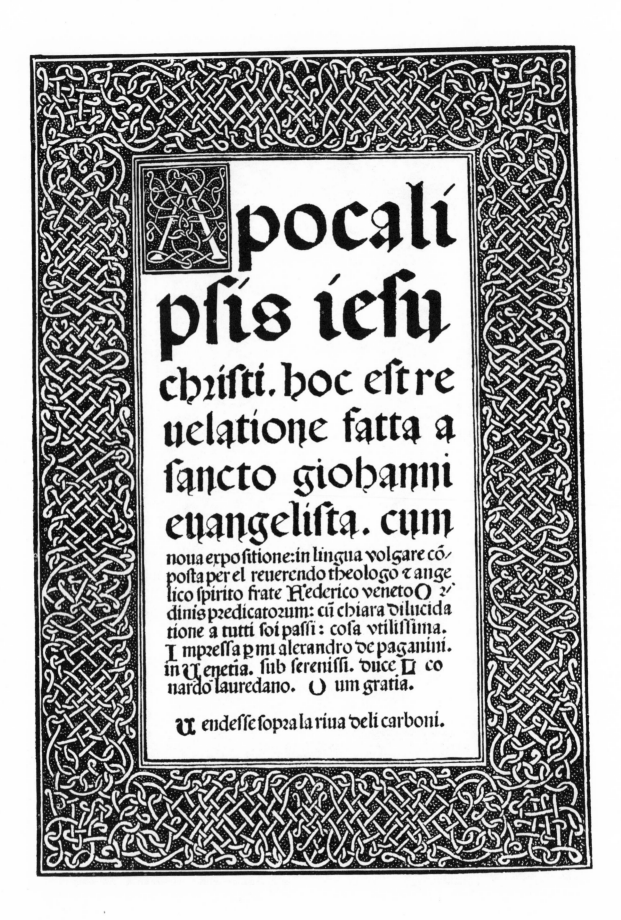

Apocalípsis iesu christi. hoc est reuelatione fatta a sancto giohanni euangelista. cum noua expositione: in lingua volgare cóposta per el reuerendo theologo τ angelico spirito frate Federico veneto Ordinis predicatorum: cũ chiara dilucidatione a tutti soi passi: cosa vtilissima. Impressa p mi alexandro de paganini. in Venetia. sub serenissi. duce Lconardo lauredano. Cum gratia.

Uendesse sopra la riua deli carboni.

Ornamented title page printed by Alessandro Paganino / VENICE 1515

PSALTERIVM
IN QVATVOR
LINGVIS
HEBRAEA
GRAECA
CHALDAEA
LATINA.

IMPRESSVM
COLONIAE
MDXVIII.

Ornamented title page from a Psalterium / COLOGNE 1518

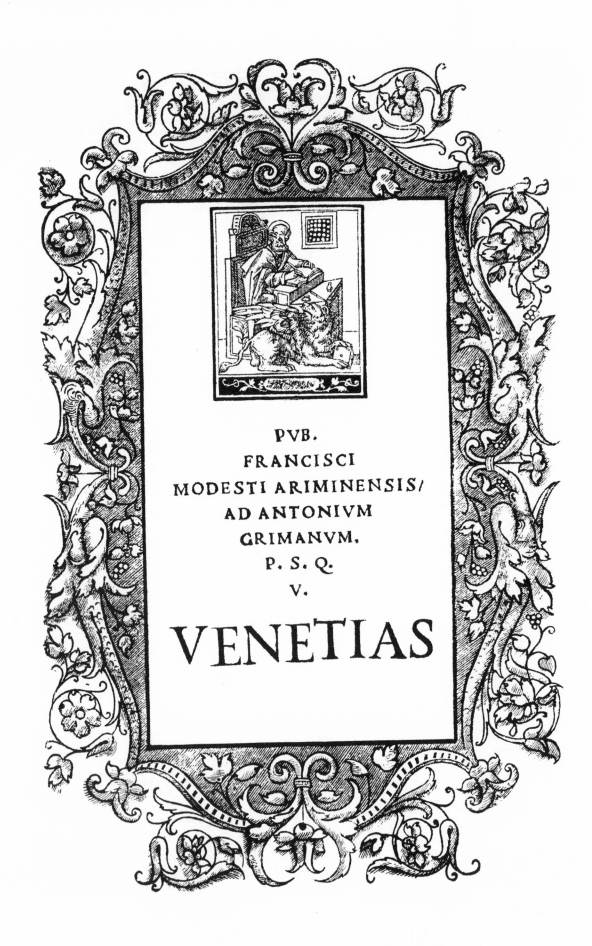

PVB.
FRANCISCI
MODESTI ARIMINENSIS/
AD ANTONIVM
GRIMANVM.
P. S. Q.
V.

VENETIAS

*Ornamented title page printed by Bernardinus de Vitalis/*VENICE 1521

Title page printed by Peter Treveris/LONDON 1527

שָׁבֻרך

הַמֵּתָר עַל הַגוֹיִם ·
אֲשֶׁר לֹא יְדָעוּךָ וְעַל
הַמַּמְלָכוֹת אֲשֶׁר
בְּשִׁמְךָ לֹא
קָרָאוּ ·

שְׁפֹךְ עֲלֵיהֶם זַעְמְךָ וַחֲרוֹן
אַפְּךָ יַשִׂיגֵם תִּרְדֹּף בְּאַף
וְתַשְׁמִידֵם מִתַּחַת שְׁמֵי יְיָ

Hebrew title page printed by Gerson Cohen / PRAGUE 1527

Tetraſtichon Authoris.
Florida diuinæ quiſquis ſecreta matheſis
Scire cupis,facili mente fruare decet:
Nam licet aſſiduo poſſis ſuperare labore,
Mens generoſa tamen plurima ſola capit.
FINIS.

End page from the first mathematical book by Oronce Finé / PARIS 1530

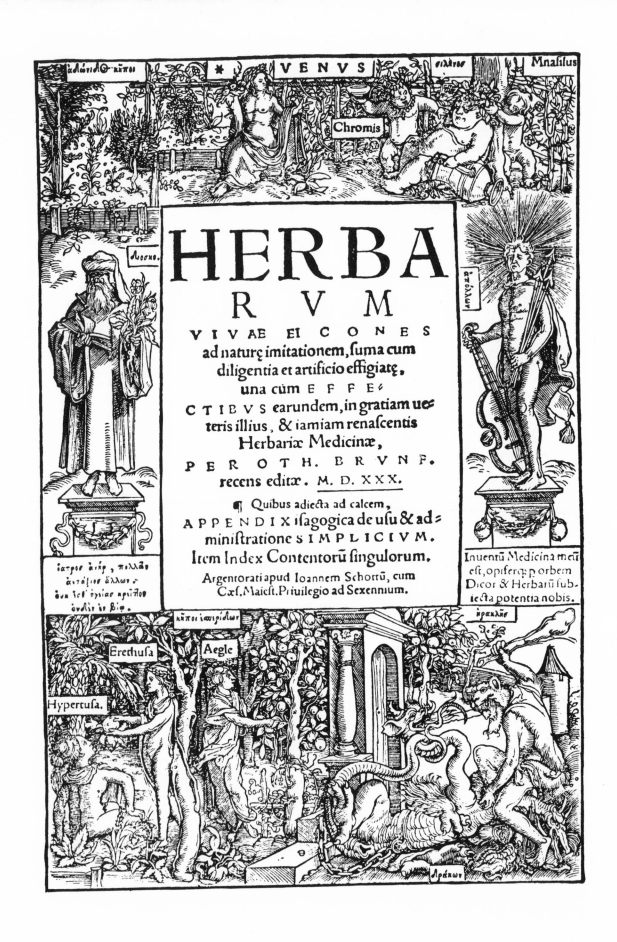

Title page designed by Hans Weiditz/STRASBOURG 1530

Pantagruel.

Les horribles et espouéta/
bles faictz & prouesses du tresrenômé
Pantagruel Roy des Dipsodes/
filz du grand geât Gargan-
tua/Côposez nouuelle;
ment par maistre
Alcofrybae
Nasier.

❧ On les vend a Lyon en la maison
de Claude nourry/dict le Prince
pres nostre dame de Confort.

Der CXLVII.
Psalm Lauda
Jerusalem.
Außgelegt durch
D. Mart. Luther.

Wittemberg.

M.D.XXXII.

Ornamented title page printed by Fridrich Peypus / NUREMBERG 1532

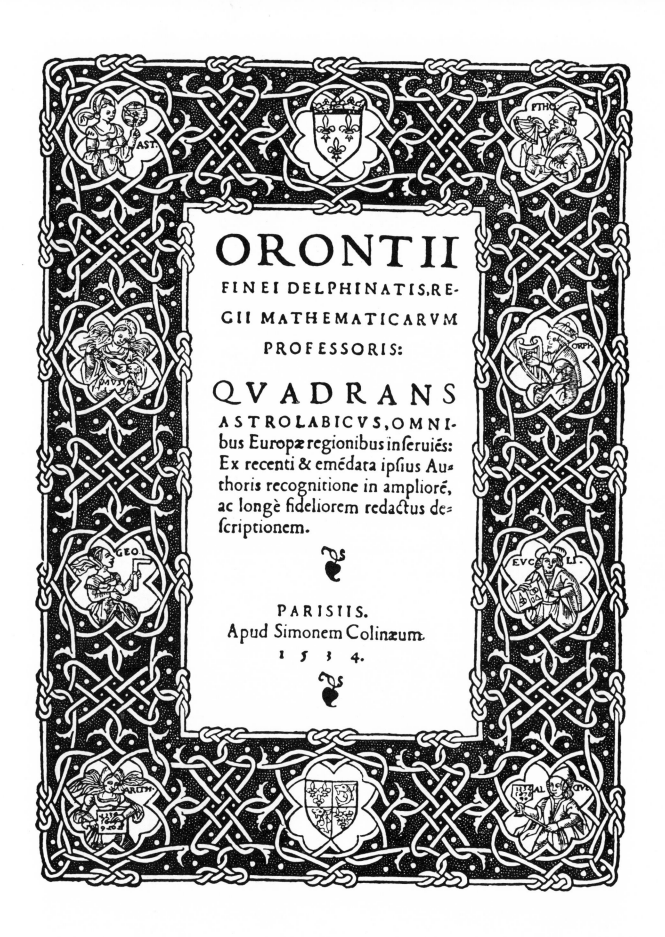

ORONTII

FINEI DELPHINATIS, RE-
GII MATHEMATICARVM
PROFESSORIS:

QVADRANS

ASTROLABICVS, OMNI-
bus Europæ regionibus inferuiés:
Ex recenti & emédata ipfius Authoris recognitione in amplioré,
ac longè fideliorem redactus de=
fcriptionem.

PARISIIS.
Apud Simonem Colinæum.
1 5 3 4.

Ornamented title page designed by Oronce Finé / PARIS 1534

Title page printed by Rychard Grafton / LONDON 1540

King Henry the eyght.

End page printed by Rychard Grafton / LONDON 1548

BIBLIA.
DAS IST,
DIE GANTZE
HAILIGE SCHRIFFT
VERDEVTSCHET
DVRCH.
D. MARTIN.
LVTTER.

GEDRVCKT ZV.
WITTENBERG.
ANNO.
MDLVIII

Title page designed by Virgil Solis/WITTENBERG 1558

Title page designed by Jost Amman / FRANKFORT O.M. 1570

Title page printed by Christoph Plantin / ANTWERP 1578

THE
COVNTESSE
OF PEMBROKES
ARCADIA.

WRITTEN BY SIR
PHILIP SIDNEY
Knight.

NOW THE FOVRTH TIME
PVBLISHED, WITH SVNDRY
NEW ADDITIONS OF THE
same Author.

LONDON
Imprinted for MATHEW LOVVNES
Anno DOMINI.
1605.

Title page printed for Mathew Lownes / LONDON 1605

THE
Decameron
CONTAINING
An hundred pleasant
Nouels.

*Wittily difcourfed, betweene
feauen Honourable Ladies, and
three Noble Gentle-
men.*

London, printed by
Ifaac Iaggard,
1620.

Title page printed by Isaac Iaggard/LONDON 1620

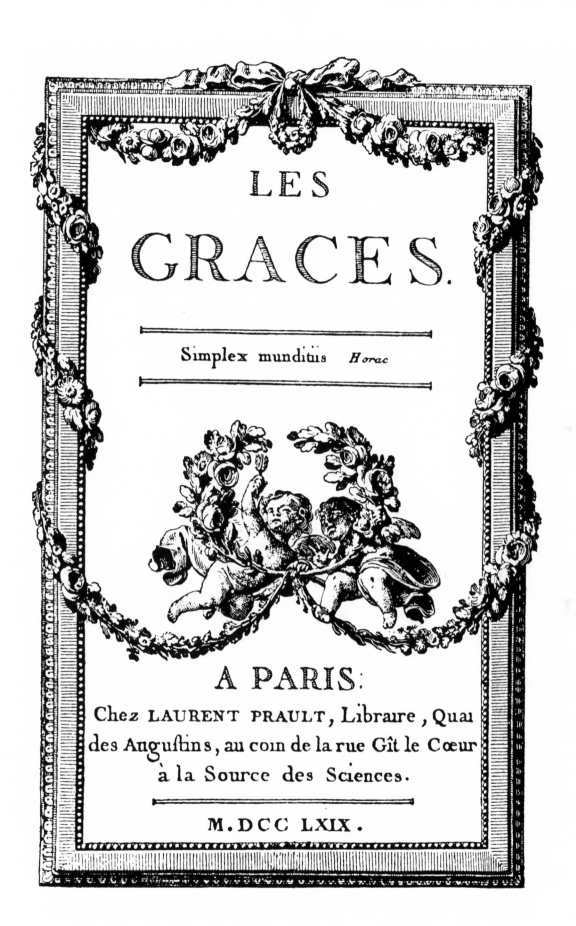

LES GRACES.

Simplex munditiis   *Horac*

A PARIS:

Chez LAURENT PRAULT, Libraire, Quai
des Auguſtins, au coin de la rue Gît le Cœur
à la Source des Sciences.

M.DCC LXIX.

Title page designed by Jean-Michel Moreau the Younger / PARIS 1769

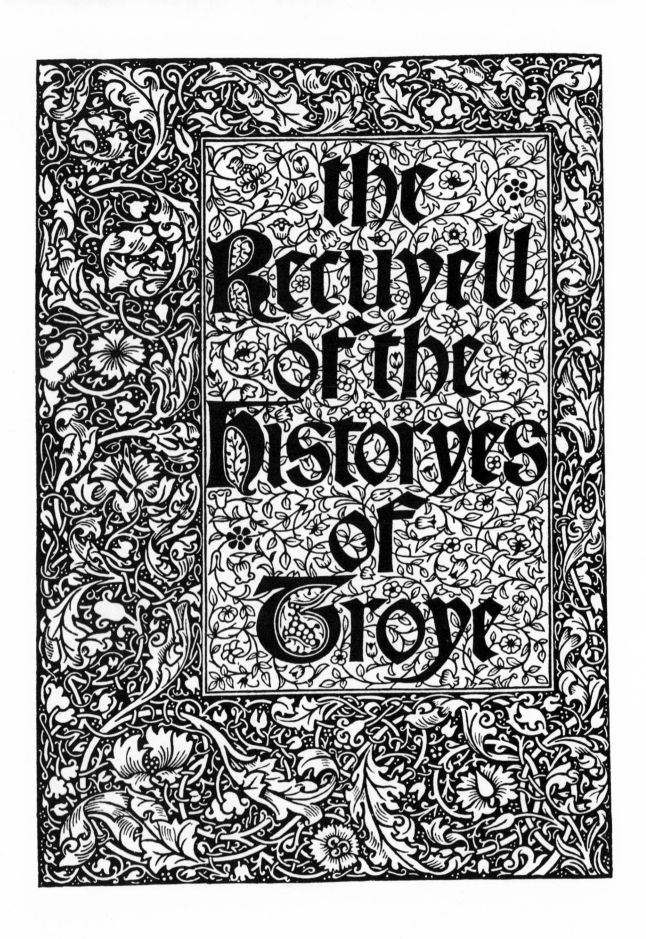

Title page designed by William Morris, Kelmscott Press / HAMMERSMITH 1892

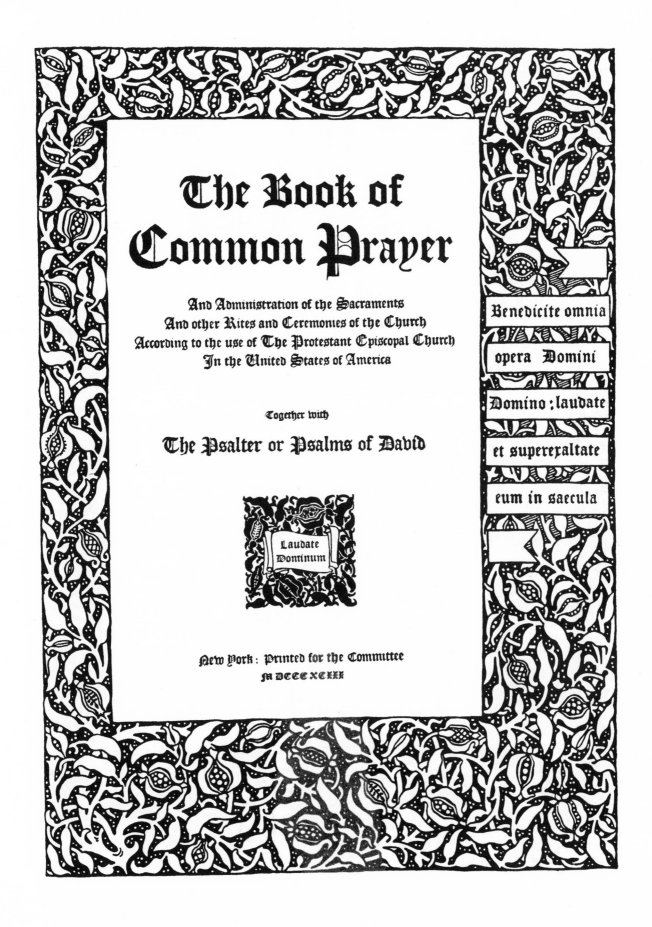

The Book of Common Prayer

And Administration of the Sacraments
And other Rites and Ceremonies of the Church
According to the use of The Protestant Episcopal Church
In the United States of America

Together with

The Psalter or Psalms of David

Laudate Dominum

Benedicite omnia
opera Domini
Domino : laudate
et superexaltate
eum in saecula

New York : Printed for the Committee
M DCCC XCIII

Title page designed by Bertram G. Goodhue, De Vinne Press / NEW YORK 1893

Title page designed by Koloman Moser, Staatsdruckerei/VIENNA 1904

LETTERS & ALPHABETS

Initial B from a manuscript / TOLEDO 11TH CENTURY

LETTERS AND ALPHABETS

PAGE 57
Initial B from a manuscript, Toledo 11th century.

PAGE 59
Initial K from a manuscript, Germany 12th century.

PAGE 60
Ornamented Hebrew letters from incunabula, printed by Joshua Salomon Soncino, Cremona 1483.

' PAGE 61
Ornamented alphabet, England 1490.

Ornamented alphabet, Germany 15th century.

PAGES 62–63
Greek initials from "Etymologicum Magnum", printed by Zacharias Callierges, Venice 1499.

PAGES 64–65
Initials from incunabula, Paris–Lyons 1485–1499.

PAGES 66–67
Children alphabet by Hans Weiditz, Augsburg 1521.

PAGE 68
Ribbon alphabet from Ludovico Vicentino's "Regolo da imparare scrivere", printed by Nicolo Zoppino, Venice 1533.

Ornamented alphabet from Juan de Yciar's "Arte subtilissima", Saragossa 1550.

PAGE 69
Ornamented alphabet by Daniel Hopfer, Nuremberg 1549.

Monograms from Juan de Yciar's "Arte subtilissima", Saragossa 1550.

PAGES 70–71
Initials from Juan de Yciar's "Arte subtilissima", Saragossa 1550.

PAGE 72
Initials from Amphiareo Vespasiano's "Opera", Venice 1554.

PAGE 73
Alphabet from Giovanni Francesco Cresci's "Il perfetto Scrittore", Rome 1569.

PAGE 74
Title page and human alphabet from Johann Theodor and Johann Israel De Bry's "Alphabeta et Characteres", Frankfort o.M. 1596.

PAGE 75
Ornamented alphabet, Italy 16th century.

PAGES 76–77
Initials from Lucas Kilian's "Newes A B C Büchlein", Augsburg 1627.

PAGE 78
Initials from Johann Daniel Preisler's "Orthographia", printed by Johann Christoph Weigl, Nuremberg about 1700.

PAGE 79
Calligraphic alphabet from Mánoel Andrade de Figueiredo's "Nova Escola", Lisbon 1722.

PAGE 80
Ornamented alphabet, Austria 18th century.

PAGE 81
Wood alphabet from Joseph Balthazar Silvestre's "Alphabet Album", Paris 1843.

PAGE 82
Animal alphabet from Joseph Balthazar Silvestre's "Alphabet Album", Paris 1843.

LETTERS AND ALPHABETS

DURING THE fifth and the sixth centuries, monastic scribes for the early church began to give the first letter on the first page of their manuscripts a greater prominence. These enlarged letters were called "Initials" from the Latin *initialis* meaning "beginning."

In the many ecclesiastic and worldly manuscripts of the following centuries, these initials became larger and more ornamented; embellished with pictorial décor and miniature illustrations; adorned with designs in gold and illuminated with brilliant colors. Such initials were used not only as the first letter of a manuscript but also at the beginning of divisions, chapters, paragraphs and even sentences. Through the extensive use of these elaborately ornamented initials in medieval times, they became an integral part of early book decoration.

When Johannes Gutenberg designed his Bible, he had to take into consideration that his printed books must compete with these manuscripts of rich décor. Ornamented initials were accepted as an absolutely necessary and indispensable feature of a well-made and attractive book. So Gutenberg and his successors used the movable ornamented initial in their printed works in an outstanding way and with excellent results.

From this time on throughout the last five hundred years, nearly every known and unknown woodcutter, engraver, writing master, illustrator, type designer, punch-cutter and printer made his contribution to the uncountable multitude of ornamented initials and alphabets.

Initial K from a manuscript / GERMANY 12TH CENTURY

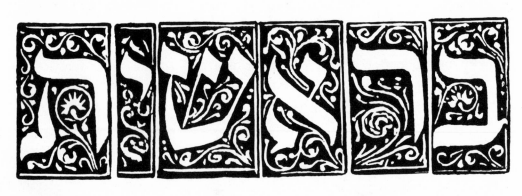

Ornamented Hebrew letters by Joshua Salomon Soncino / CREMONA 1483

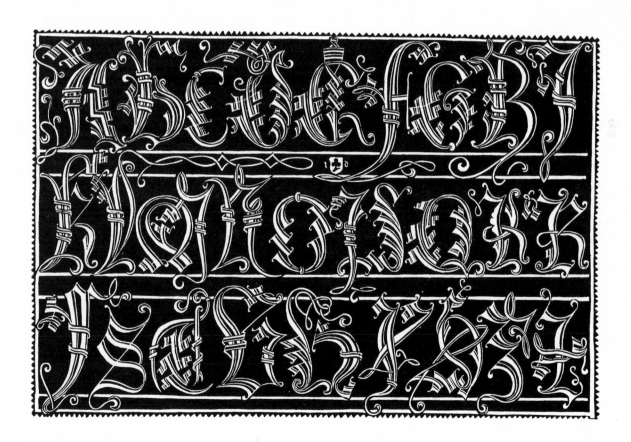

Ornamented alphabet / ENGLAND 1490

Ornamented alphabet / GERMANY 15TH CENTURY

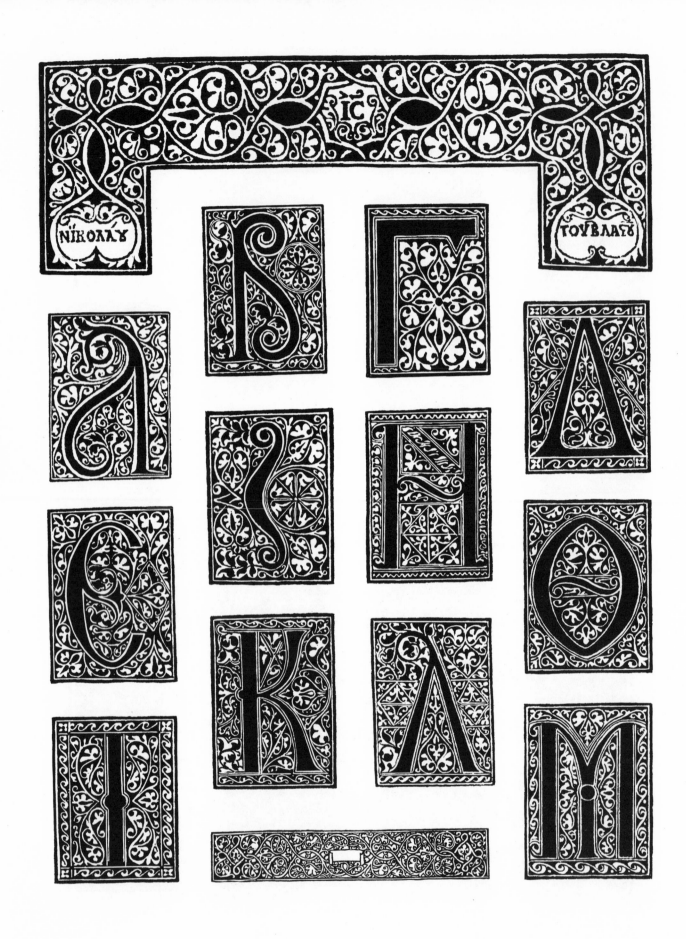

Greek initials by Zacharias Callierges / VENICE 1499

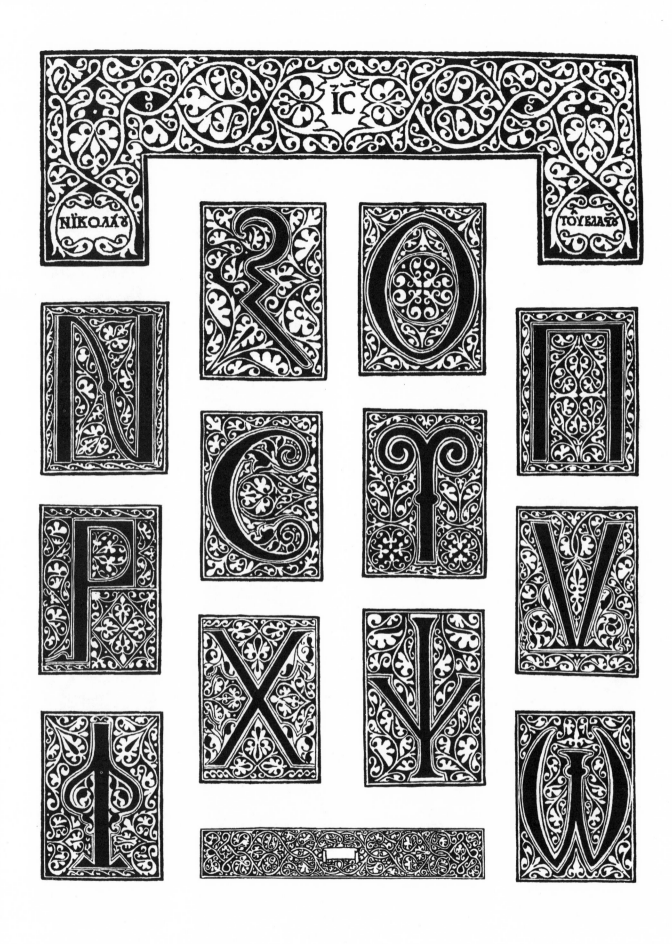

Greek initials by Zacharias Callierges / VENICE 1499

Initials from incunabula / PARIS-LYONS 1485–1499

Initials from incunabula / PARIS-LYONS 1485–1499

·65·

Children alphabet by Hans Weiditz/AUGSBURG 1521

Children alphabet by Hans Weiditz/AUGSBURG 1521

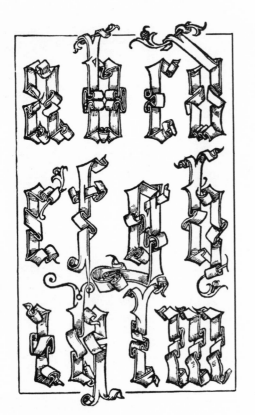
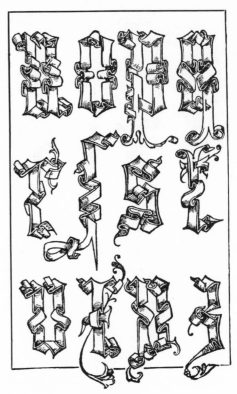

Ribbon alphabet by Ludovico Vicentino / VENICE 1533

Ornamented alphabet by Juan de Yciar / SARAGOSSA 1550

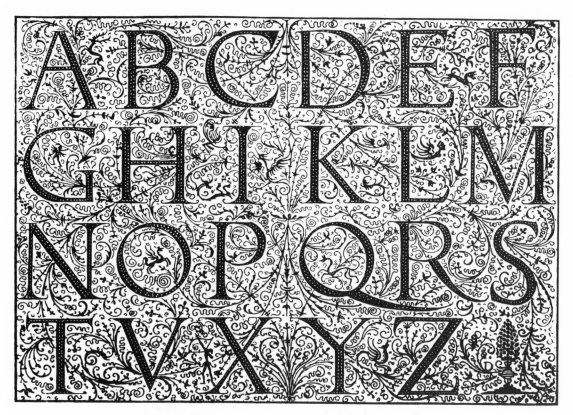

Ornamented alphabet by Daniel Hopfer / NUREMBERG 1549

Monograms by Juan de Yciar / SARAGOSSA 1550

Initials by Juan de Yciar / SARAGOSSA 1550

Initials by Juan de Yciar/SARAGOSSA 1550

Calligraphic initials by Amphiareo Vespasiano / VENICE 1554

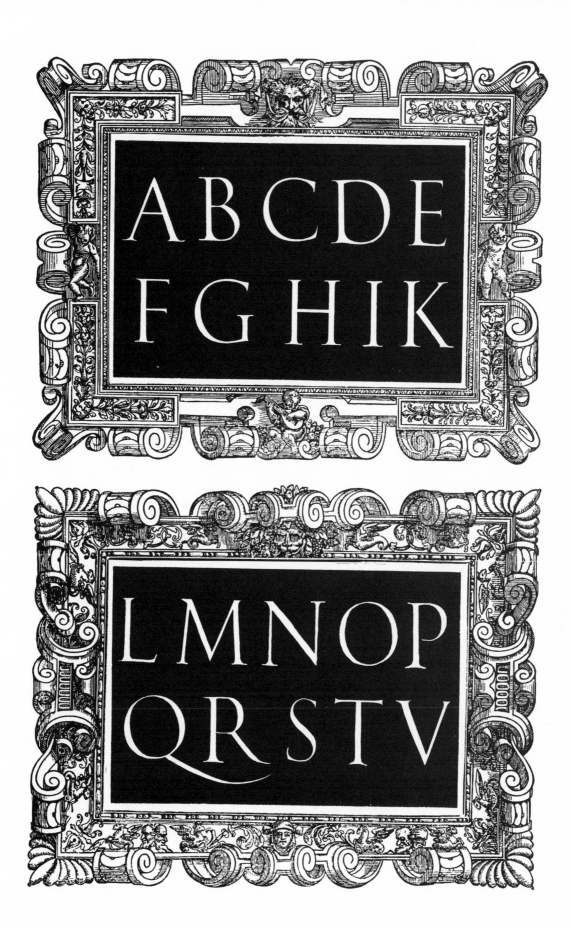

Alphabet by Giovanni Francesco Cresci / ROME 1569

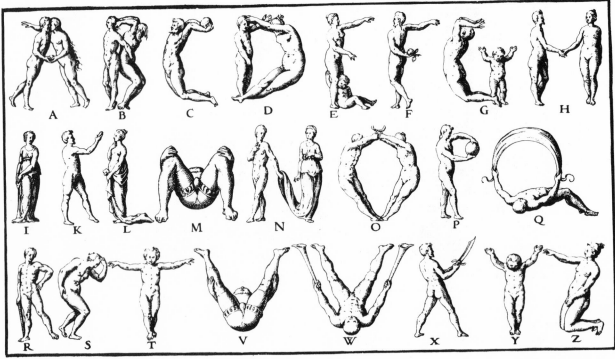

*Human alphabet by Jo. Theodor and Jo. Israel De Bry/*FRANKFORT O.M. 1596

Ornamented alphabet / ITALY 16TH CENTURY

Initials by Lucas Kilian / AUGSBURG 1627

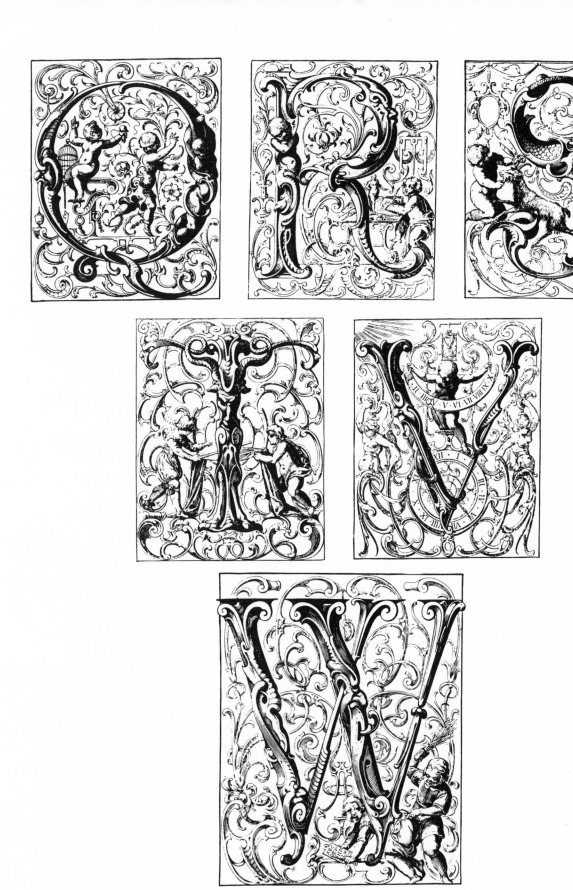

Initials by Lucas Kilian / AUGSBURG 1627

Initials by Johann Daniel Preisler / NUREMBERG ABOUT 1700

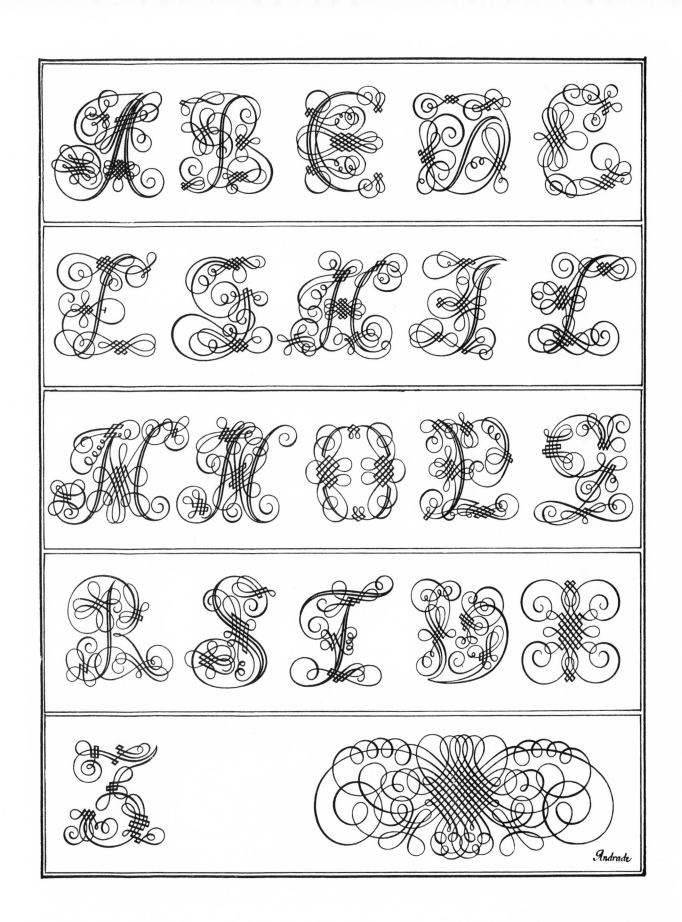

Calligraphic alphabet by Mánoel Andrade de Figueiredo / LISBON 1722

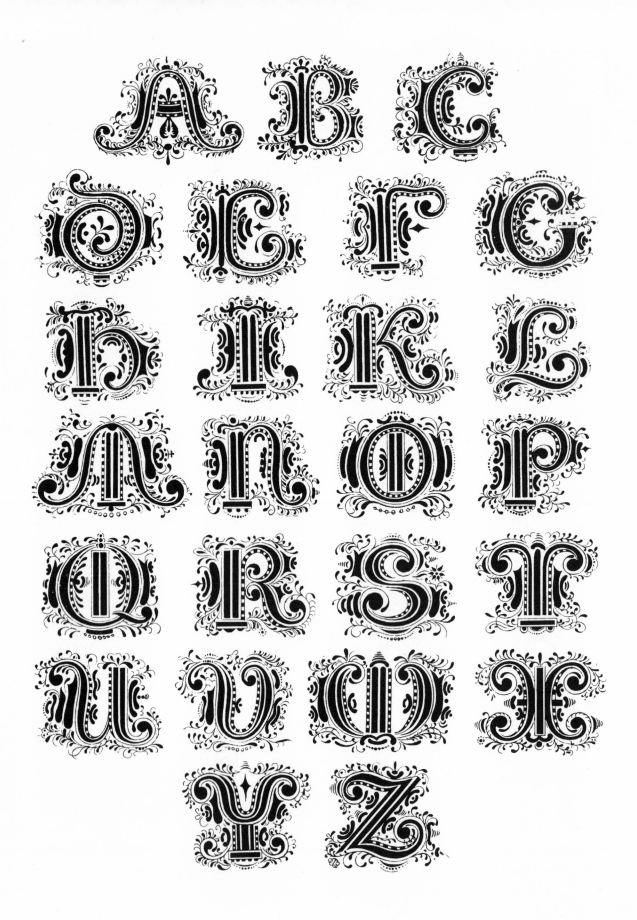

Ornamented alphabet / AUSTRIA 18TH CENTURY

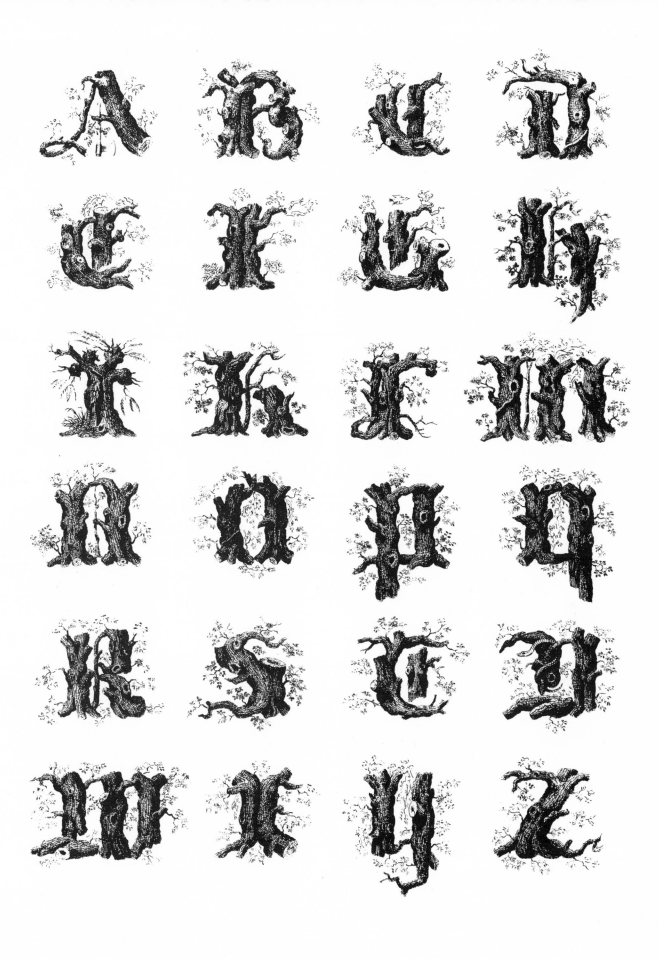

Wood alphabet by Joseph Balthazar Silvestre / PARIS 1843

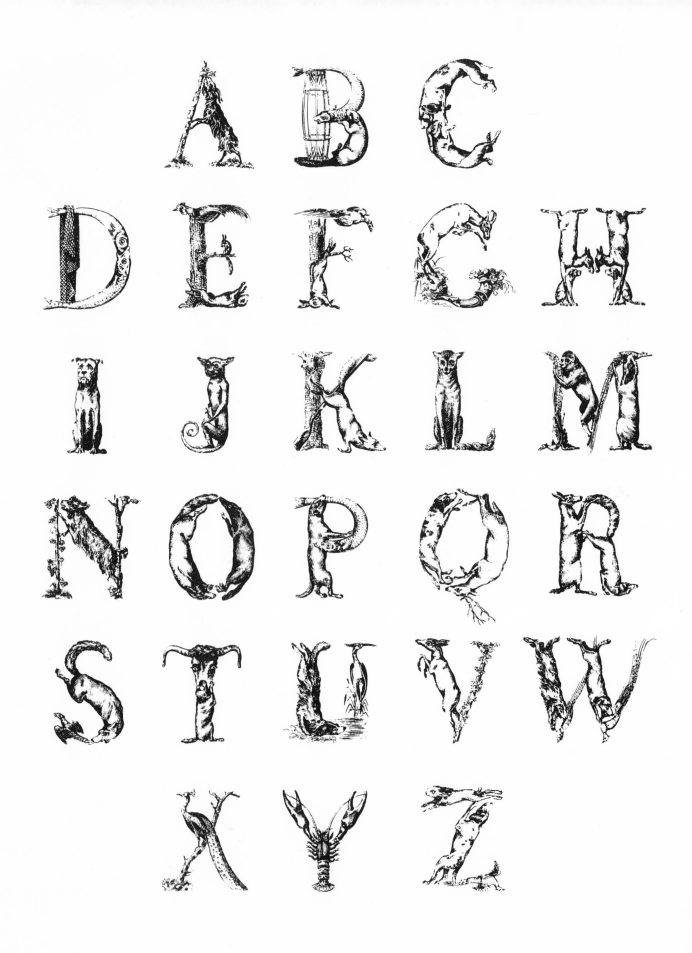

Animal alphabet by Joseph Balthazar Silvestre / PARIS 1843

Fleurons & Borders

RVBRICA

ALNOME DEL NOSTRO
SIGNORE
IESV CHRISTO
E DELA
SVA GLORIOSA MADRE
SEMPRE
VERZENE MARIA
COMENCIA VNO BELLO
TRACTATO
ALA CREATVRA MOLTO
VTILE
ET ANCI NECCESSARIO
CIOE
DELA SCIENTIA ET
ARTE
DE BEN MORIRE
ET BEN
FENIRE LA VITA
SVA

*The first "Fleurons" printed by Giovanni and Alberto Alvise/*VERONA 1478

FLEURONS AND BORDERS

PAGE 83

The first "Fleurons" from "Arte de ben morire", printed by Giovanni and Alberto Alvise, Verona 1478.

PAGE 85

Typographic ornaments by William Caslon Jr., from Philip Luckombe's "The History and Art of Printing", London 1771.

PAGES 86–87

Title page, typographic borders and ornaments from Georg Wolffger's "Format Büchlein", Graz 1670.

PAGE 88

Typographic borders and ornaments from Louis René Luce's "Épreuve du premier alphabet", printed by L'Imprimerie Royale, Paris 1740.

PAGE 89

Typographic anniversary broadside "Jubilaeum Typographicum", Erfurt 1740.

PAGE 90

Typographic title pages from Pierre-Simon Fournier's "Modéles des Caractères", Paris 1742 and "Manuel Typographique", Paris 1764–1766.

PAGE 91

Typographic ornaments from Pierre-Simon Fournier's "Modéles des Caractères", Paris 1742.

PAGE 92

Title page from Loyson et Briquet's "Épreuve des Caractères", Paris 1751.

Title page from Johann Thomas Trattner's "Abdruck von Röslein und Zierrathen", Vienna 1760.

Title page from Johannes Enschedé's "Proef van Letteren", Haarlem 1768.

PAGE 93

Typographic ornaments from Johann Thomas Trattner's "Abdruck von Röslein und Zierrathen", Vienna 1760.

PAGE 94

Typographic colophons by C. and A. Adibert, Aix 1767–1773.

PAGE 95

Title page from Joseph Gillé's "Épreuves des caractères", Paris 1773.

Title page from Johann Joseph Engel's "Specimen Characterum", Pecs-Fünfkirchen 1773.

Title page from Isaiah Thomas' "A Specimen of Printing Types", Worcester, Mass. 1785.

PAGE 96

Typographic ornaments (First Empire), Paris 1810–1819.

PAGE 97

Typographic borders (Restauration), Paris 1820–1829.

PAGES 98–99

Typographic borders and ornaments from "Probeblätter", by Andreäische Buchhandlung, Frankfort o.M. 1838.

PAGE 100

Typographic borders by A. Beyerhaus, Berlin 1840.

PAGE 101

Typographic border (Louis Philippe), Paris 1840–1849.

PAGE 102

Typographic borders (Cathedral), Paris 1840–1849.

PAGE 103

Typographic title page by John T. White, New York 1843.

PAGE 104

Typographic borders (Second Empire), Paris 1860–1869.

PAGE 105

Typographic border by Farmer, Little & Co., New York 1873.

PAGE 106

Typographic borders and ornaments (Second Renaissance), Berlin 1870–1890.

FLEURONS AND BORDERS

THIRTY YEARS after Johannes Gutenberg invented movable printing type, two printers in Verona named Giovanni and Alberto Alvise designed movable ornaments called "Flowers" or "Fleurons." Their first book with flower decorations and borders, *Arte de ben Morire*, was printed in 1478. This book created an uproar of indignation among their fellow printers, because contemporary craftsmen and critics predicted that this infamous commercialization of book décor would eventually lead to the complete decay of the art of printing and book decoration.

Contrary to that prediction, the design of flowers and borders became, in the following centuries, a subtle and highly esteemed art in itself. All leading type-founders and punch-cutters made their special contributions to the art of movable ornaments.

In the eighteenth century, the casting of flowers reached an all-time peak. Well known type designers and founders, like Louis René Luce and Pierre-Simon Fournier, Jr., in Paris, Johann Thomas Trattner in Vienna, Johannes Enschedé in Haarlem, William Caslon, Jr., in London, and many others were vying for the laurel with their artistic flower and border designs.

The nineteenth century brought on a flood of flower specimens, good and bad, artistic and commercial, new creations and crude imitations. And so at the turn of the century, after almost 450 years, the prediction of the critics in Verona became a near reality. The art of book décor and printing, with the exception of the work of a few bibliophilistic diehards, was drowned in commercialization.

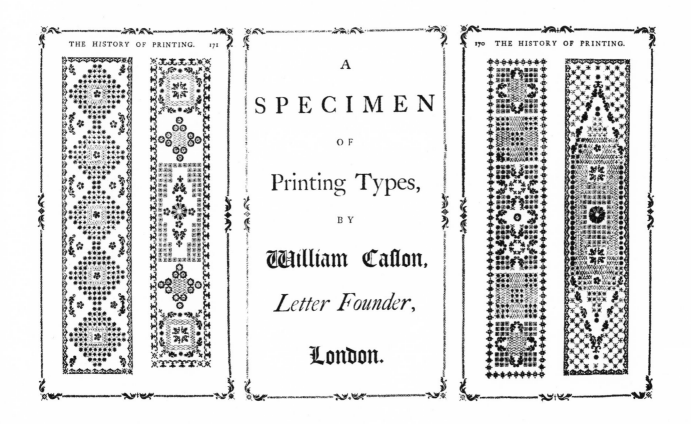

Typographic ornaments by William Caslon, Jr./ LONDON 1771

New-Auffgesetztes
* * * * * * * * * * * * * * * * * * * *
FOrmat-Büchlein/
Darinnen abgesetzte Figuren/ wie man die Columen
außschiessen soll/ in allen gemeinen Formaten/
mit sambt deren Abtheilungen/
Allen
Der Löblichen Buchdruckerey-Kunst Erfahrnen/
besonders denen Setzer-Gesellen/ vnd Lehrjungen/
gantz nutzlich vnd befürderlich zugebrauchen/ weilen es
nicht alles in Gedächtnuß kan behalten werden/
In der Landsfürstlichen Haupt-Statt Grätz/ in den Druck gegeben/
Von
Georgen Wolffger/ B. G.

1670.

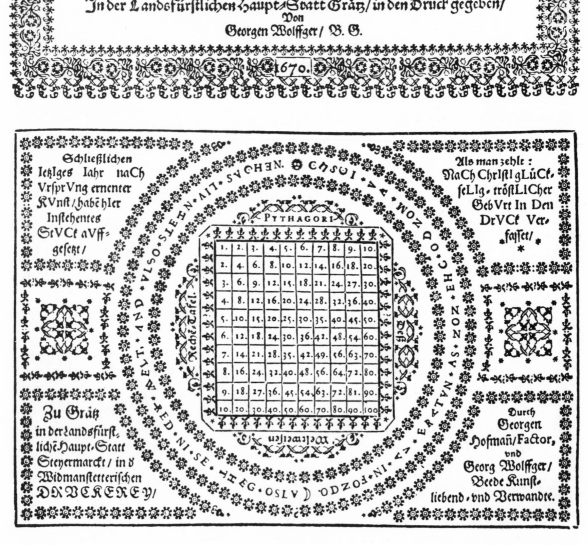

Typographic borders by Georg Wolffger / GRAZ 1670

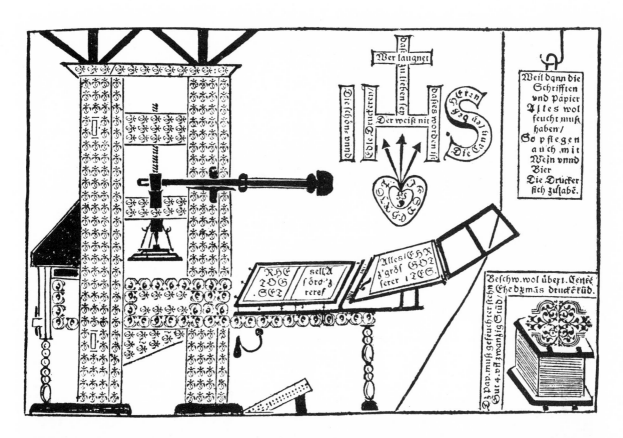

Typographic ornaments by Georg Wolffger / GRAZ 1670

Typographic borders and ornaments by Louis René Luce / PARIS 1740

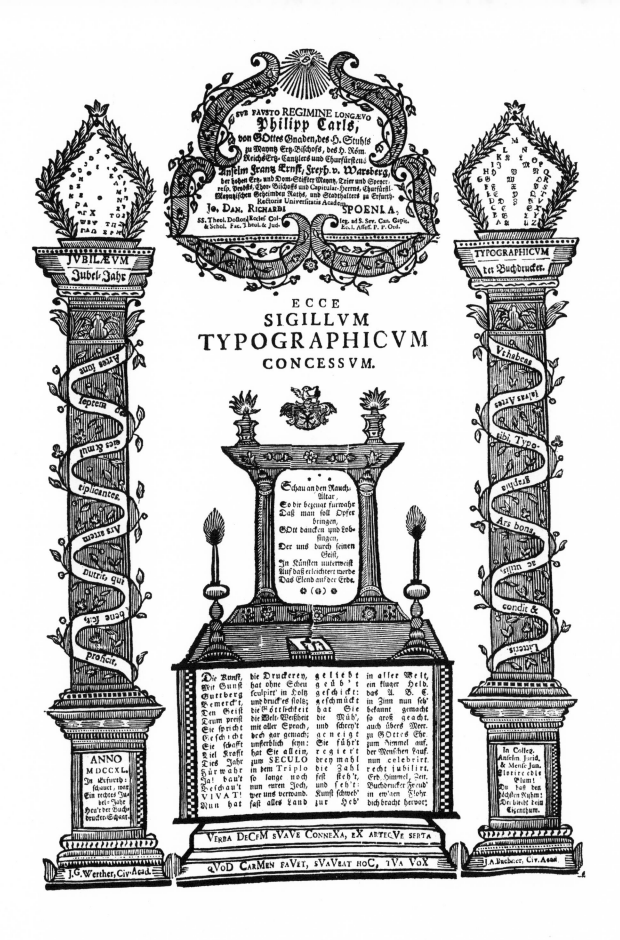

Typographic anniversary broadside/ERFURT 1740

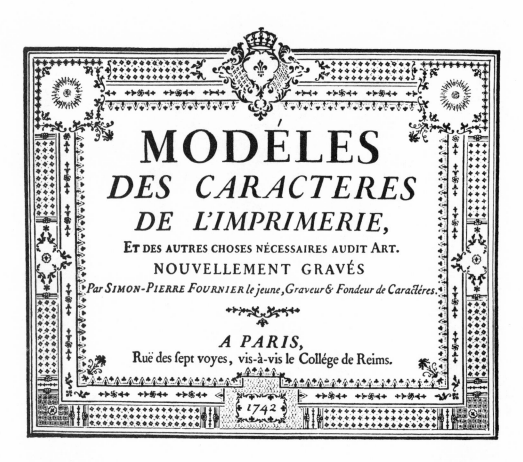

MODÉLES
DES CARACTERES
DE L'IMPRIMERIE,
ET DES AUTRES CHOSES NÉCESSAIRES AUDIT ART.
NOUVELLEMENT GRAVÉS
Par SIMON-PIERRE FOURNIER le jeune, Graveur & Fondeur de Caractéres.

A PARIS,
Ruë des sept voyes, vis-à-vis le Collége de Reims.

1742

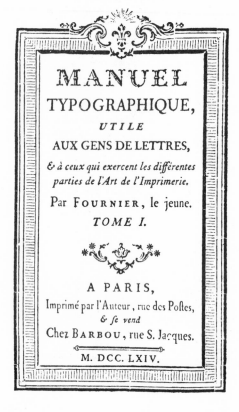

MANUEL
TYPOGRAPHIQUE,
UTILE
AUX GENS DE LETTRES,
*& à ceux qui exercent les différentes
parties de l'Art de l'Imprimerie.*

Par FOURNIER, le jeune.

TOME I.

A PARIS,
Imprimé par l'Auteur, rue des Poftes,
& se vend
Chez BARBOU, rue S. Jacques.

M. DCC. LXIV.

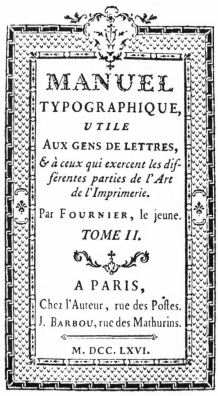

MANUEL
TYPOGRAPHIQUE,
UTILE
AUX GENS DE LETTRES,
*& à ceux qui exercent les dif-
férentes parties de l'Art
de l'Imprimerie.*

Par FOURNIER, le jeune.

TOME II.

A PARIS,
Chez l'Auteur, rue des Poftes.
J. BARBOU, rue des Mathurins.

M. DCC. LXVI.

*Title pages by Pierre-Simon Fournier, Jr./*PARIS 1742–1766

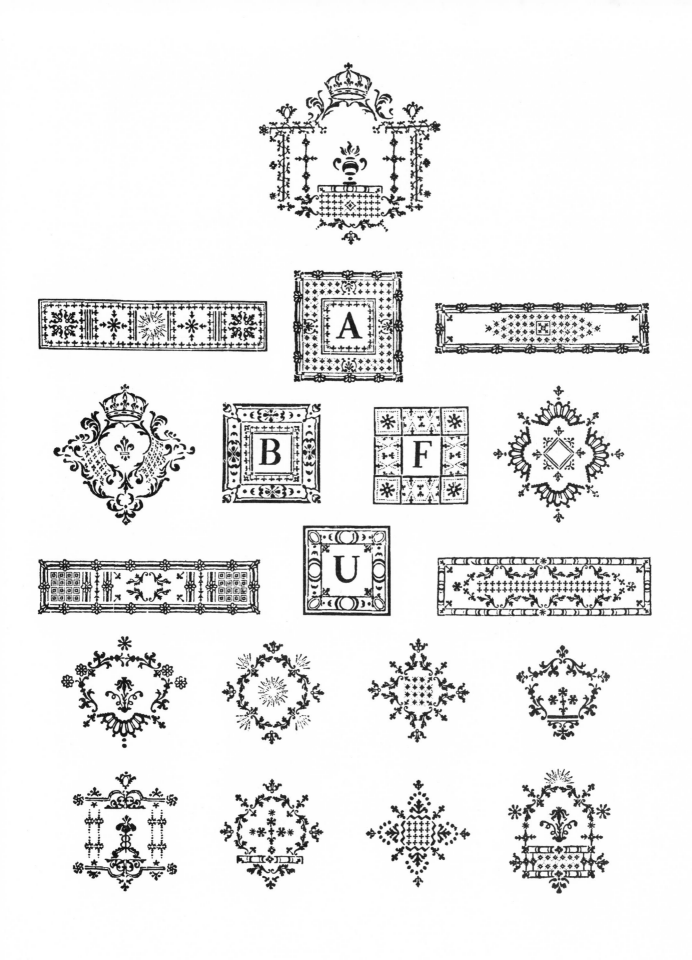

*Typographic ornaments by Pierre-Simon Fournier, Jr./*PARIS 1742

·91·

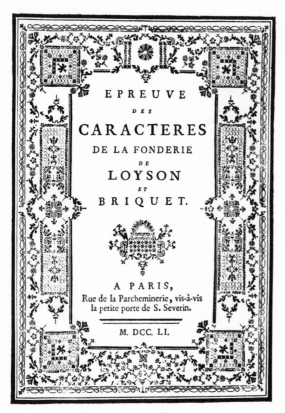

Title page by Loyson & Briquet / PARIS 1751

Title page by J. Th. Trattner / VIENNA 1760

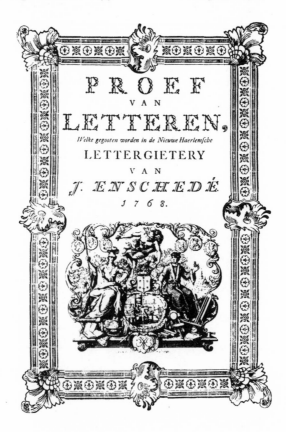

Title page by Johannes Enschedé / HAARLEM 1768

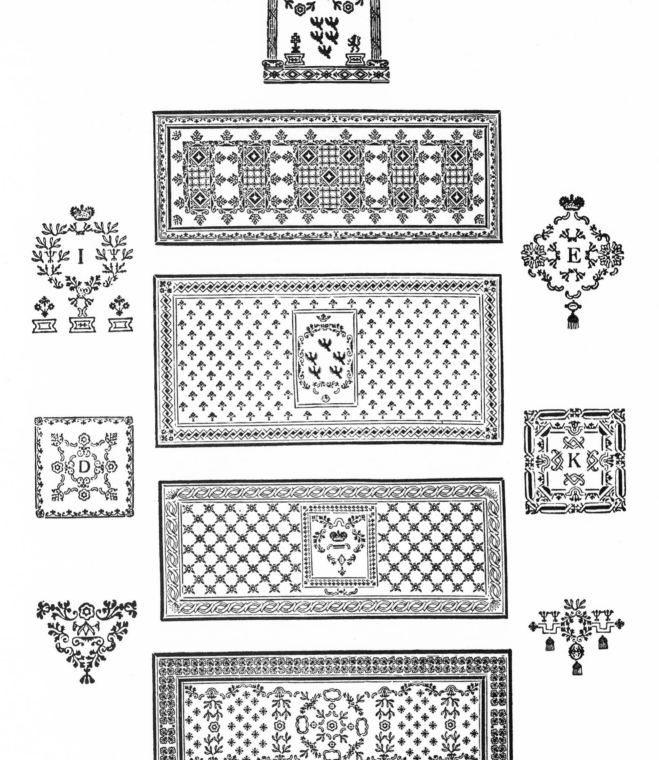

Typographic ornaments by Johann Thomas Trattner / VIENNA 1760

Typographic colophons by C. & A. Adibert / AIX 1767–1773

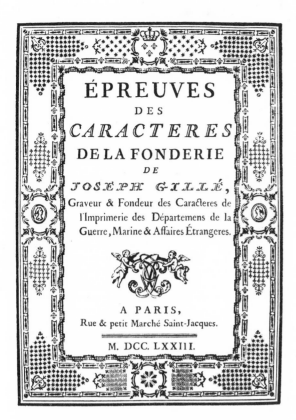

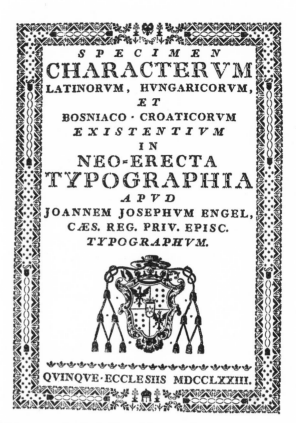

Title page by Joseph Gillé/PARIS 1773   *Title page by J. J. Engel*/PECS-FÜNFKIRCHEN 1773

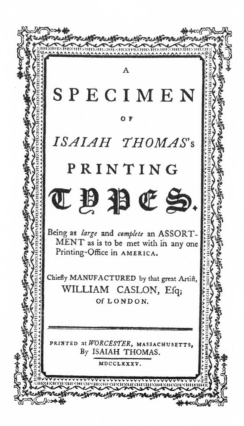

Title page by Isaiah Thomas/WORCESTER, MASS. 1785

Typographic ornaments (First Empire)/PARIS 1810–1819

Typographic borders (Restauration) / PARIS 1820–1829

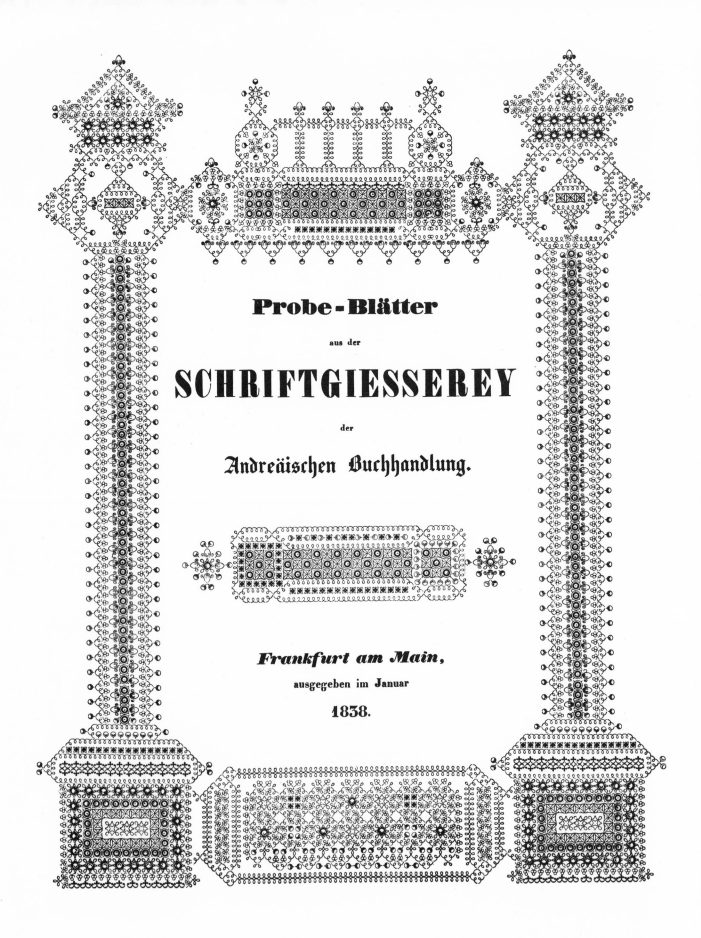

Probe-Blätter

aus der

SCHRIFTGIESSEREY

der

Andreäischen Buchhandlung.

Frankfurt am Main,

ausgegeben im Januar

1838.

Typographic border by Andreäische Buchhandlung / FRANKFORT O.M. 1838

Typographic ornaments by Andreäische Buchhandlung / FRANKFORT O.M. 1838

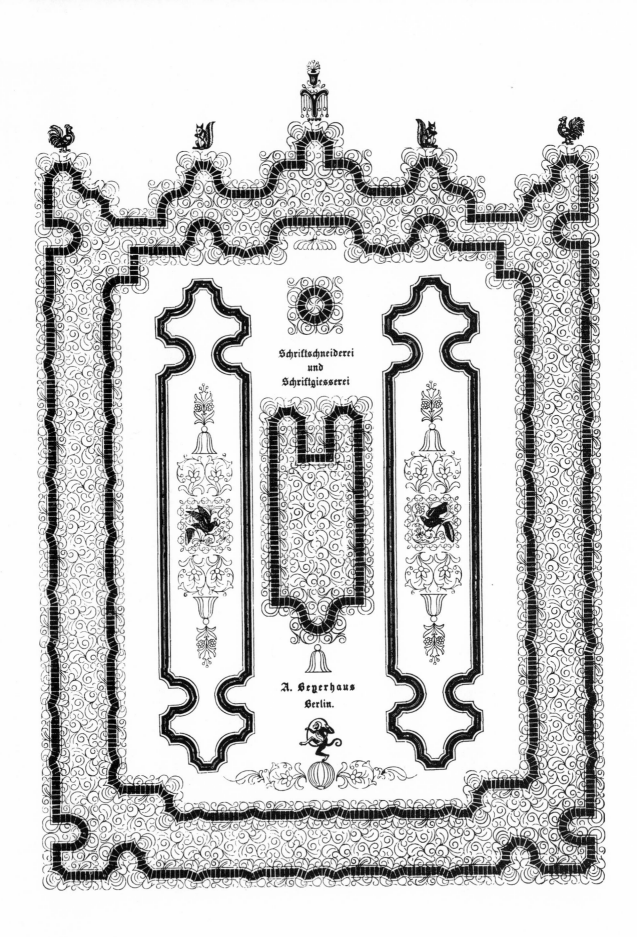

Schriftschneiderei
und
Schriftgiesserei

A. Beyerhaus
Berlin.

Typographic borders by A. Beyerhaus / BERLIN 1840

Typographic borders (Louis Philippe) / PARIS 1840–1849

Typographic borders (Cathedral) / PARIS 1840–1849

JOHN T. WHITE,

TYPE AND STEREOTYPE FOUNDER,

No. 45 Gold-street,

(SECOND DOOR SOUTH OF FULTON-STREET,)

New-York,

Invites the attention of Editors and Printers generally to his
extensive and unrivalled assortment of

TYPE, FLOWERS

AND

ORNAMENTS,

ALSO

BRASS RULES, CHASES, GALLEYS, CASES,
COMPOSING STICKS, INK,

And every article required in a Printing Office.

He is also Agent for the Napier, Smith, Washington, and
Adams' and Ramage's Power and Hand PRESSES.

ALL OF WHICH CAN BE FURNISHED AT SHORT NOTICE.

The reputation of this Foundry is believed to be fully es-
tablished, having been founded upward of thirty years, and
reference is confidently made to many of the leading jour-
nals of the United States and the Canadas as to the beauty
and durability of the Type.

Orders put up for the South American and Mexican mar-
kets, with Spanish, French and Portuguese Accents.

Editors and Printers wishing to establish a Newspaper
or Job Printing Office, will be furnished with an estimate
in detail for the same, by stating the size of the paper, or
the particular style and quantity of work to be executed.

1843.

Title page by John T. White/ NEW YORK 1843

Typographic borders (Second Empire) / PARIS 1860–1869

Typographic border by Farmer, Little & Co./ NEW YORK 1873

Typographic borders (Second Renaissance) / BERLIN 1870–1890

Headpieces & Vignettes

Calligraphic endpiece from a manuscript / PARIS 15TH CENTURY

HEADPIECES AND VIGNETTES

PAGE 107

Calligraphic endpiece from a manuscript, Paris 15th century.

PAGE 109

Headpieces and vignettes printed by Aldus Manutius from "Aristophanis Comoediae novem", Venice 1495 and from "Hypnerotomachia Poliphili", Venice 1499.

PAGE 110

Vignettes by Hans Holbein the Younger from "The Pastyme of People", printed by John Rastell, London 1529.

PAGE 111

Headpieces printed by the first Russian printer Ivan Fedorov, from "The Apostles of LwóW", Moscow 1564 and from the "Ostrog Bible", Ostrog 1580.

PAGES 112–113

Head- and endpieces printed by Denys Thierry, Augustin Courbé, L'Imprimerie Royale and others, Paris 1630–1670.

PAGE 114

Headpieces from Jean Mabillon's "De re diplomatica", printed by Vicentii Ursini, Naples 1681.

PAGE 115

Head- and endpieces from Johann Gabriel Doppelmayr's "Historische Nachricht von den Nürenbergischen Mathematicis und Künstlern", printed by Johann Ernst Adelbulner, Nuremberg 1730.

PAGE 116

Head- and endpieces by Stephan Mack, Sigmund Calles and others, Vienna 1740–1750.

PAGE 117

Head- and endpieces by Sigmund Calles, Vienna 1750–1760.

PAGES 118–119

Endpieces and vignettes by Jean Baptiste Michel Papillon and others, from Specimenbooks printed by L'Imprimerie Royale and L'Imprimerie Nationale, Paris 1760–1799.

PAGES 120–121

Vignettes from "Proben der Polytypen" by J. Ritchel von Hartenbach, Jr., Erfurt 1836.

PAGE 122

Vignettes by Aubrey Beardsley, printed by Kelmscott Press, Hammersmith 1891–1895.

HEADPIECES AND VIGNETTES

HEADPIECES, endpieces and vignettes, as well as flowers and initials, played an important part in the decoration of printed books. Headpieces were put at the beginning of a book and its chapters; endpieces, called tailpieces or *cul-de-lamp*, were used at the end of the book or at its divisions; vignettes or emblems were scattered throughout a book wherever the typographer wanted to use a decorative spot.

To determine the exact origin of most of these decorations, it would be necessary to check such designs contained in every rare book in every library and collection all around the globe. It would be necessary to check their publishing dates and places as well as their printers. It would be an impossible task.

The fact that the same design was sometimes used simultaneously or only a few years apart in the most distant locations, makes it impossible to pinpoint the exact time and origin of most of these decorations. The type-founders who originated this kind of book ornament sold and resold such cuts to faraway places. Not even the specimen books of the early foundries give absolute proof of origin, because it was customary for type-cutters and printers to include in their specimen books their whole stock, without reference to their own or foreign make or time of design.

The assignment of most of these decorations to a certain artist, printer or country is partly guesswork, based in many instances only on special style elements, make-up or technical considerations.

Headpieces and vignettes by Aldus Manutius/VENICE 1495–1499

Vignettes by Hans Holbein the Younger / LONDON 1529

Headpieces by Ivan Fedorov / MOSCOW-OSTROG 1564–1580

Head- and endpieces / PARIS 1630–1650

Head- and endpieces / PARIS 1650–1670

Headpieces by Vicentii Ursini / NAPLES 1681

Head- and endpieces by Johann Ernst Adelbulner / NUREMBERG 1730

Head- and endpieces / VIENNA 1740–1750

Head- and endpieces by Sigmund Calles / VIENNA 1750–1760

Endpieces and vignettes by L'Imprimerie Royale / PARIS 1760–1789

Head- and endpieces by L'Imprimerie Nationale / PARIS 1792–1799

Vignettes by J. Ritchel von Hartenbach, Jr./ERFURT 1836

*Vignettes by J. Ritchel von Hartenbach, Jr./*ERFURT 1836

· 121 ·

Vignettes by Aubrey Beardsley, Kelmscott Press/HAMMERSMITH 1891–1895

SILHOUETTES & SHADOW FIGURES

Silhouette / INDIA

SILHOUETTES AND SHADOW FIGURES

PAGE 123
Silhouette, India.

PAGE 125
Silhouettes, peasant art, Russia 19th century.

PAGE 126
Shadow pictures from the hero play "Nang Talung", Siam.

PAGE 127
Shadow picture from the Indian hero play "Ramayana", Siam.

PAGE 128
Shadow figures, Siam.
Putra, the prince and Angada, the son of the king of the apes.

PAGE 129
Shadow figures, Siam.
Mandodari, the princess of the demons and the hero from "Nang Talung".

PAGE 130
Heads from shadow puppets, China.
Tschô Wang, last emperor of the Yin dynasty and Yü Po-Ya.

PAGE 131
Heads from shadow puppets, China.
Hsieh-Li and Tng Tsch'an-Yü.

PAGE 132
Shadow puppets, Bali.

PAGE 133
Intermission sign from a shadow play, Java.

PAGES 134–135
Shadow puppets, Java.

PAGE 136
Shadow puppets, Turkey.
The Drunkard, Hadchwad and the Dwarf.

PAGE 137
Shadow play figures, Mameluke, Egypt 14th century.

PAGES 138–139
Lantern silhouettes, China.

PAGES 140–141
Silhouette stencils for silk and cotton printing, Shijo-Kioto, Japan.

PAGE 142
Silhouette "Calvary", Holland about 1700.

PAGE 143
Silhouettes, peasant art, Italy 18th century.

PAGE 144
Silhouettes by an unknown Viennese artist, Austria 18th century.

PAGE 145
Silhouettes, monks' art, Germany 19th century.

PAGE 146
Silhouettes by Jean Jacob Hauswirth, Basel 1860.

SILHOUETTES AND SHADOW FIGURES

SINCE TIMES of old, human beings were intrigued by an unbelievable bodiless phenomenon around them, the shadow. Everywhere black shadows waxed and waned, painting grotesque shapes and figures on everything. No wonder that the creative mind of man used light and shadow as an artistic and decorative medium.

Shadow art is not an expression of a single period, a definite territory or a certain people. Shadow painting and shadow decoration came and went throughout all ages and all continents, like the medium itself, anywhere and everywhere.

The use of shadow art is evidenced in applied art from all four corners of the globe. We see it in Egyptian hieroglyphs and Etruscan vase paintings. In tribal symbols and decorations in Africa, North and South America. In shadow puppets in the Far and Middle East. In silhouette portraits and wall paintings, shadow figures and ornaments for lanterns and light shades, pottery and basket décor. In Russian Tula silver and Moresque metal etching, and scores of other objects.

The expression "Silhouette" is comparatively new. It was coined in France in 1759 for cheap and easily produced articles after the name of the French minister of finance of that time, Étienne de Silhouette. The term was used in mockery of his stern and unpopular economy laws.

Silhouettes, peasant art / RUSSIA

Shadow play picture / SIAM

Shadow play picture / SIAM

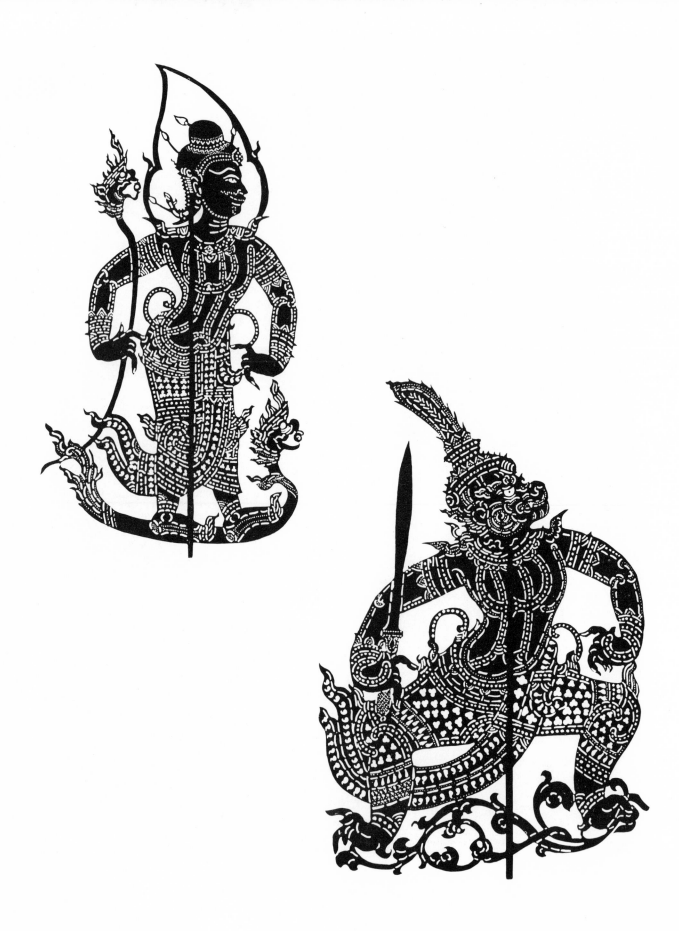

Shadow play figures / SIAM

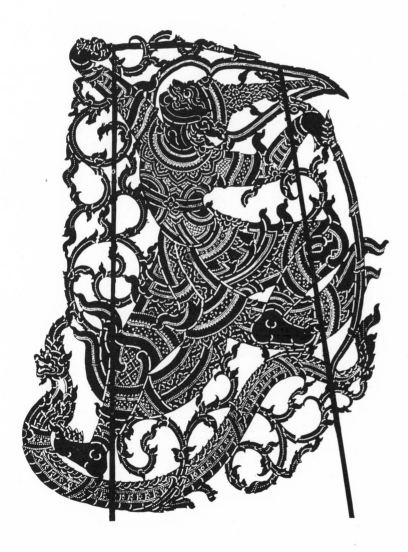

Shadow play figures/SIAM

Heads from shadow puppets / CHINA

Heads from shadow puppets / CHINA

Shadow puppets / BALI

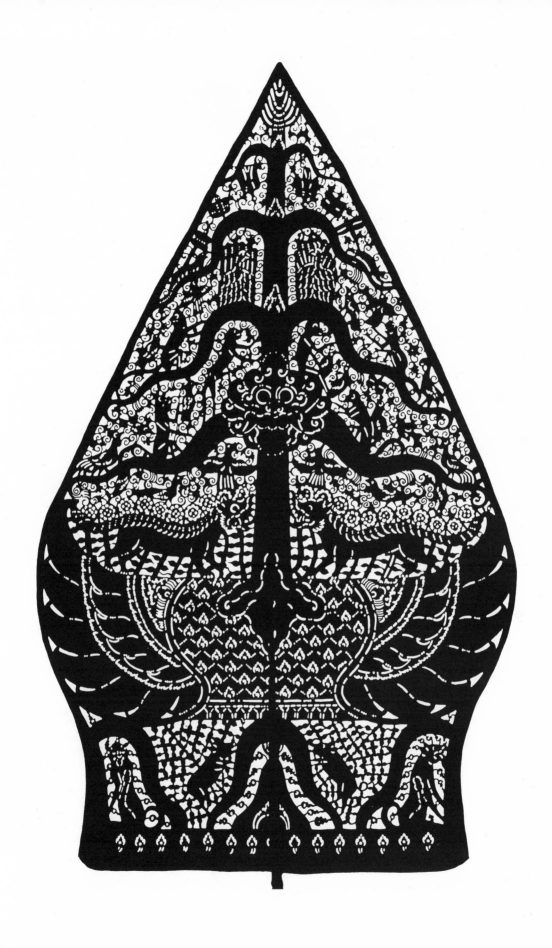

Intermission sign from a shadow play / JAVA

Shadow puppets / JAVA

Shadow puppets / JAVA

Shadow puppets/TURKEY

Shadow play figures, Mameluke / EGYPT 14TH CENTURY

Lantern silhouettes / CHINA

Lantern silhouettes / CHINA

Stencils for silk printing / JAPAN

Stencils for silk printing / JAPAN

Silhouette "Calvary" / HOLLAND ABOUT 1700

Silhouettes, peasant art/ITALY 18TH CENTURY

Silhouettes/VIENNA 18TH CENTURY

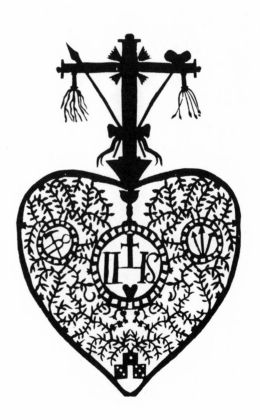

Silhouettes, monks art / GERMANY 19TH CENTURY

Silhouettes by Jean Jacob Hauswirth / BASEL 1860

APPLIED ORNAMENTS &
PATTERN BOOKS

Calligraphic ornament from a manuscript / ENGLAND 12TH CENTURY

APPLIED ORNAMENTS AND PATTERN BOOKS

PAGE 147

Calligraphic ornament from a "Bestiarium," England 12th century.

PAGE 149

Centre-pieces from Francisco Columna's "Hypnerotomachia Polophili", printed by Aldus Manutius, Venice 1499.

PAGES 150–151

Needlepoint patterns by Albrecht Dürer, Nuremberg 1505.

PAGES 152–153

Monstrances from Lucas Cranach's "From Dye zaigung des hochlobwirdigen hailigthums", Wittenberg 1509.

PAGES 154–155

Title page, frontispiece and lace designs from Alessandro Paganino's "Il burato libro de recami", Venice 1518.

PAGES 156–157

Embroidery and lace designs from Nicolo Zoppino's "Essemplario di lavori", Venice 1529.

PAGES 158–159

Title page and embroidery designs from Francisque Pellegrin's "Lafleur de la science de Pourtraicture", Paris 1530.

PAGES 160–161

Title page and embroidery designs from Peter Quentel's "Eyn newe kunstlich moetdelboeck", Cologne 1532.

PAGE 162

Title page and lace design from Giovanni Andrea Vavasore's "Essemplario di lavori", Venice 1532.

PAGE 163

Lace designs from Mattheo Pagan's "Giardinetto novo di punti tagliati", Venice 1543.

PAGES 164–165

Metal etching designs from Peter Flötner's "Maureskenbuch", printed by Rudolph Wyssenbach, Zurich 1546.

PAGE 166

Embroidery designs from Giovanni Ostaus' "La vera perfettione del disegno di varie sorte di Ricami", Venice 1567.

PAGE 167

Title page and lace designs from Giacomo Franco's "Nuova inventione de diverse mostre," Venice 1596.

PAGES 168–169

Title page and lace designs from Hans Sibmacher's "Schön Neues Modelbuch", printed by Balthaser Xaimoyen, Nuremberg 1597.

PAGES 170–171

Title page and lace designs from Iaques Foillet's "Nouveaux pourtraicts de Point coupé", Montbeliard 1598.

PAGES 172–173

Title page, frontispieces and lace designs from Federic de Vinciolo's "Les singuliers et nouveaux pourtraicts d'ouvrages de Lingeries", Paris 1606.

PAGE 174

Designs for earrings by the Dutch goldsmith Master P. R. K., Holland 1609.

PAGE 175

Title page and wrought iron work designs from Hugues Brisville's "Diverses pieces de Serruriers", engraved by Jean Berain, Paris 1663.

PAGE 176

Design for metal etching, sword hilt and scabbard, by Antoine Jacquard, Poitiers first half 17th century.

PAGE 177

Engraving designs for plaques from Henri Janssen's "The four elements", Amsterdam 17th century.

PAGES 178–179

Curtain and panel designs by Daniel Marot, The Hague 1712.

PAGE 180

Crochet type by L. Johnson & Co. from "Specimens of Printing Types", MacKellar, Smith & Jordan, Philadelphia 1873.

APPLIED ORNAMENTS AND PATTERN BOOKS

ONE OF the most astounding misconceptions, found in discussions with contemporary artists and craftsmen, is the belief that the roots of regional decoration and the core of epochal styles are in the so-called "peasant art" of that special territory or period. This is an absolutely false derivation, contrary to the true occurrences.

In bygone times, peasants were serfs. Theirs and their women's hands were heavy from hard work. Their personal chattels were nil, and their shapeless garments were made from coarse fabrics. They had no skill in handicrafts and no possessions of their own worthy of embellishment.

The designing of objects of applied art—wood carvings, table ware, household implements, fashion accessories, jewelry, etc.—was the domain of leading artists and artisans. Spinning, weaving, embroidering, pearl-stitching, lace-making, etc., were the prerogatives and pastimes of the ladies of the ruling and well-to-do upper crust. The use of certain materials and fabrics, weaves and colors, lace and jewelry was an exclusive right of certain families, castes or office holders.

Only after the peasants became free men on their own land did they copy the styles and designs of their former masters and so they developed an art of their own, always far behind the contemporary style of their time and surroundings. The basic forms and designs of contemporary peasant art can be found in the pattern and model books of the leading artists and craftsmen of many centuries ago.

Center pieces by Aldus Manutius/VENICE 1499

Needlepoint pattern by Albrecht Dürer / NUREMBERG 1505

Needlepoint pattern by Albrecht Dürer / NUREMBERG 1505

Monstrances by Lucas Cranach / WITTENBERG 1509

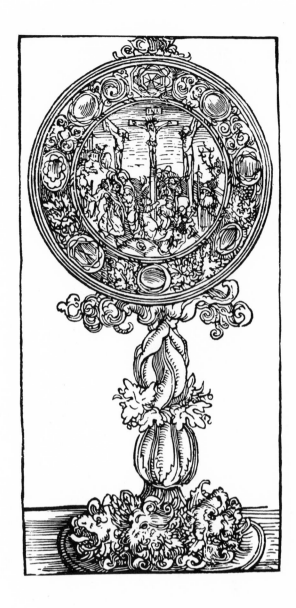

Monstrances by Lucas Cranach / WITTENBERG 1509

Lace designs by Alessandro Paganino / VENICE 1518

E auertisse con el disegno insieme ti appostiamo vn posfilo bellissi-
mo e vago e tocchio cosa non mancho da teterse cara che esso di
segno: laqual cosa da noi sono stata con grandissima fatica com-
posta e ordinata a tua vtilita e pochissima spesa.   Uale

Lace designs by Alessandro Paganino / VENICE 1518

Embroidery and lace designs by Nicolo Zoppino/VENICE 1529

Embroidery and lace designs by Nicolo Zoppino / VENICE 1529

La fleur de la science de Pourtraicture
Et patrons de broderie. Façon arabicque/et ytalique.
Cum priuilegio regis.

Embroidery designs by Francisque Pellegrin/ PARIS 1530

*Embroidery designs by Francisque Pellegrin/*PARIS 1530

Eyn newe kunstlich moetdelboech alle kunstner
zo brauchen fur snytzeller/wapensticker perlensticker.etc. vnd ouch fur Jonferen vnd
frauwen/ernstlich vff das neuwes gefondë allë den genë die vff kunstë verstät habent.
Gedruckt zo Cöllen, durch Peter Quentel. Jmiar, M..D.XXXIJ .im Bramaent.

*Embroidery designs by Peter Quentel/*COLOGNE 1532

Embroidery designs by Peter Quentel/COLOGNE 1532

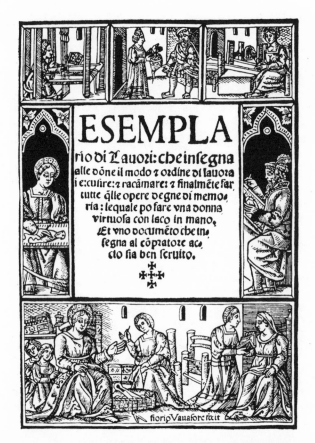

Lace design by Giovanni Andrea Vavasore/VENICE 1532

Lace designs by Mattheo Pagan/VENICE 1543

Metal etching designs by Peter Flötner / ZURICH 1546

*Metal etching designs by Peter Flötner/*ZURICH 1546

Embroidery designs by Giovanni Ostaus / VENICE 1567

Lace designs by Giacomo Franco / VENICE 1596

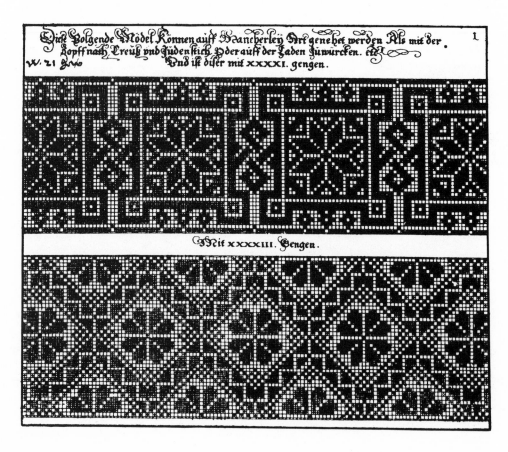

Lace designs by Hans Sibmacher / NUREMBERG 1597

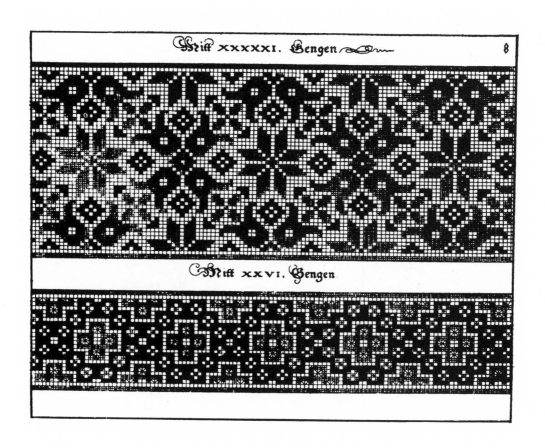

Lace designs by Hans Sibmacher / NUREMBERG 1597

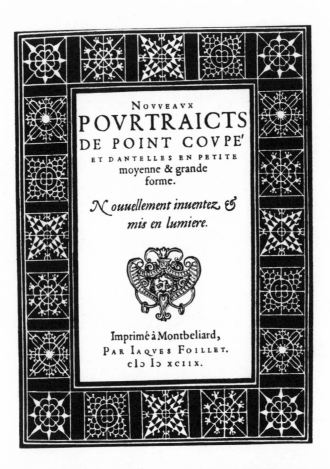

Lace designs by Iaques Foillet / MONTBELIARD 1598

Lace designs by Iaques Foillet / MONTBELIARD 1598

Trois Dieux furent parreins du troisiesme Henry,
Iupiter, Mars, Phebus; cette perle Lorraine,
Vne triple Deësse eut pour triple marreine,
Palas, Venus, la grace au chef tousiours fleury.

Peintre a fin que ton art imite la Nature,
Au tableau de ce Roy dont l'honneur touche aux Cieux,
Pein sur son chef Pallas, sur ses léures Mercure,
Mars dessus son visage, & l'amour dans ses yeux.

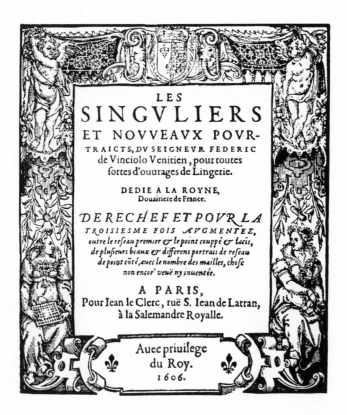

Lace designs by Federic de Vinciolo / PARIS 1606

Lace designs by Federic de Vinciolo / PARIS 1606

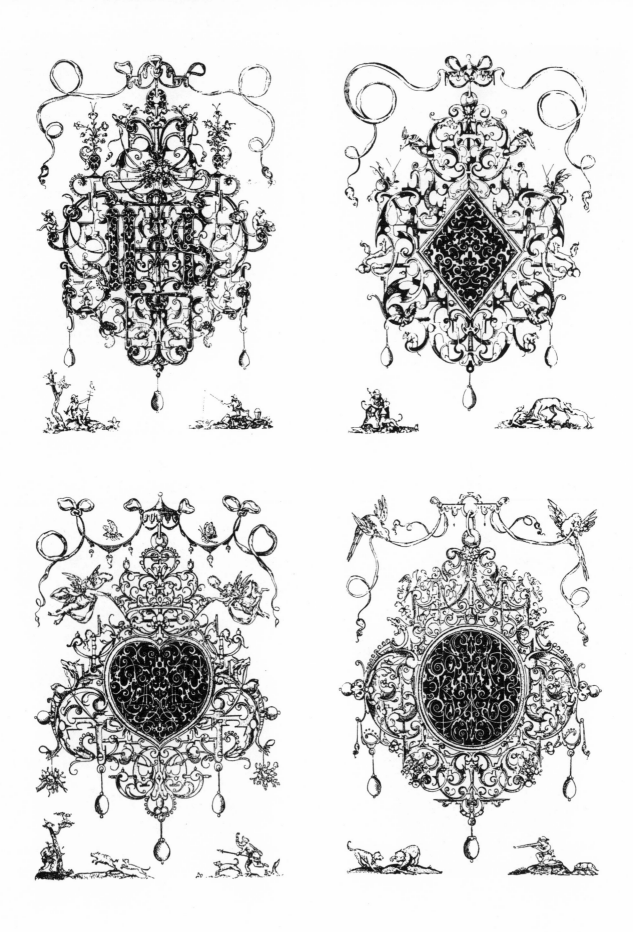

Designs for earrings/HOLLAND 1609

· 174 ·

Wrought iron work designs by Hugues Brisville / PARIS 1663

Hilt and scabbard design by Antoine Jacquard / POITIERS 17TH CENTURY

・176・

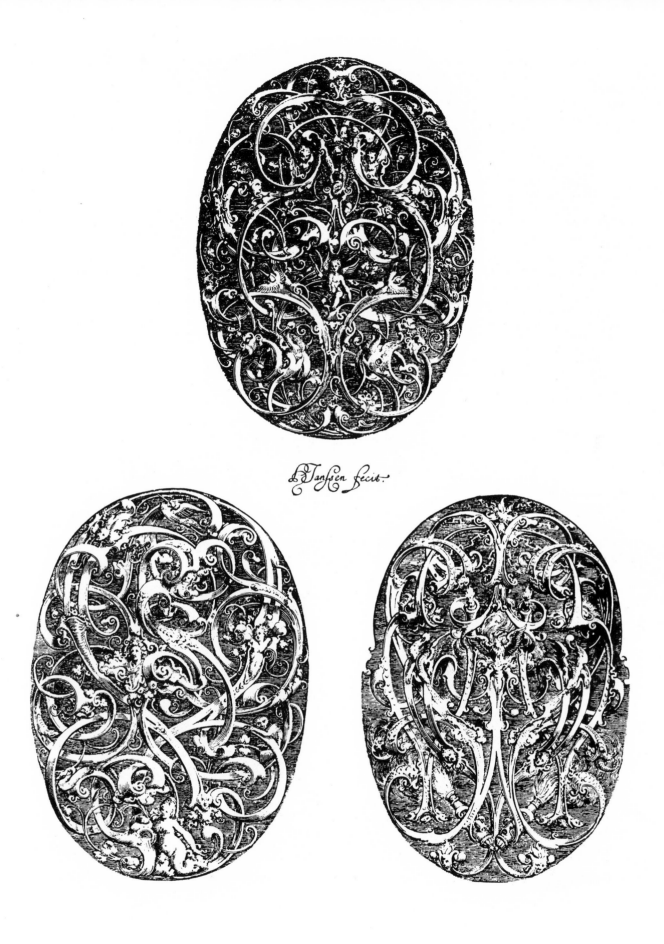

Plaque designs by Henri Janssen/AMSTERDAM 17TH CENTURY

· 177 ·

Curtain and panel designs by Daniel Marot/THE HAGUE 1712

·178·

Curtain and panel designs by Daniel Marot / THE HAGUE 1712

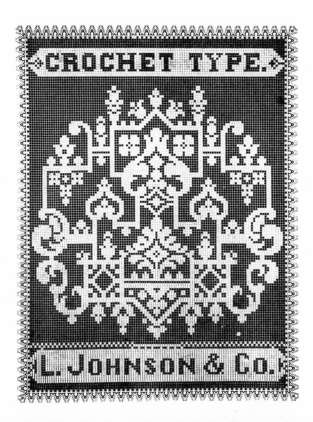

*Crochet type by L. Johnson & Co./*PHILADELPHIA 1873

Script & Scrolls

Calligraphic colophon by Peter Schöffer / PARIS 1449

PAGE 181

Calligraphic colophon by Peter Schöffer, writing master at the University of Paris, 1449.

PAGE 184

Calligraphic letter E from a manuscript (Emperor Maximilian I), Germany 15th century.

PAGE 185

Calligraphic book plates by Nicolas Flamel, writing master for Jaques le Grant, for Saint Louis IX and for the Duc de Berry, Paris 14th century.

PAGE 186

Ornamented title from "Missale Ad usum celeberrime ecclesie Eboracensis", printed by M. P. Oliveri (York-Missale), Rouen 1490.

Calligraphic title from Bartholomew de Clanville's "De Proprietate Verum", printed by Wynkyn de Worde, London 1495.

PAGE 187

Ornamented title page from Jean (Dynamantier) Duvet's "Ars Moriendi ou l'Art de bien mourir", Lyons 1496.

PAGE 188

Calligraphic title from Albrecht Dürer's "Apokalypsis", printed by Anton Koberger, Nuremberg 1498.

Calligraphic title from "Dionysii Arlopagitae caelestis hierarchia", printed by Iaccuinus de Tridino, Venice 1502.

PAGE 189

Ornamented title from "Anno Regni Regis Henrici VIII, Statutes", printed by Richard Pynson, London 1515.

Calligraphic title from Bartholomeus Zamberto's "Euclidis Megarensis philosophi platoniy", printed by Johannes Taccuinus, Venice 1517.

PAGE 190

Calligraphic title from Martin Luther's "September Testament", designed by Melchior Lotter, Wittenberg 1522.

Calligraphic page by Nicolaus Werner, Germany 16th century.

PAGE 191

Ornamented pages from Giovanni Antonio Tagliente's "La vera arte dello eccelento scrivere", Venice 1524.

PAGE 192

Title page from Sebastian Francken's "Chronica", printed by Mathias Apiarius, Bern 1539.

PAGE 193

Title page from Johann Stumpffen's "Eydgnoschaft Chronick", printed by Christoph Froschauer, Zurich 1548.

PAGES 194–195

Title page, frontispiece and calligraphic lettering from Caspar Neff's "Thesaurarium", Cologne 1549.

PAGE 196

Calligraphic broadside "Gospel", Nuremberg 1571.

PAGE 197

Title page from Jacob Jacobelln's "Fundament Buch", printed by Bernhard Jobin, Strasbourg 1579.

Ornamented page from a manuscript, Germany 16th century.

PAGE 198

Calligraphic pages from Jan van den Velde's "Spieghel der Schrijfkonste", Rotterdam 1605.

PAGE 199

Calligraphic page from De Beaugrand's "Poecilographie", Paris 1601.

Title page from Maria Strick's "Tooneel der loflijcke Schrijfpen", Delft 1607.

PAGE 200

Ornamental borders and lettering by Salomon Henrix and Petrus Bales from Hondio Judoco's "Theatrum artis scribendi", Amsterdam 1614.

PAGE 201

Calligraphic title page from Richard Gething's "Calligraphotechnia or The Art of faire writing", London 1619.

Calligraphic page from Periccioli's "Il libro della cancellaresche corsive", Siena 1619.

PAGE 202

Calligraphic scrolls from Geobattista Pisani's "Tratteggiato da Penna", Genoa 1640.

PAGE 203

Calligraphic scrolls from Edward Cocker's "The Pen's Transcendencie", London 1657.

PAGE 204

Title page from Edward Cocker's "Penna Volans", London 1661.

Title page from Edward Cocker's "Multum in Parvo", London 1672.

PAGE 205

Calligraphic scrolls from John Seddon's "The pen-mans paradise", London 1695.

PAGE 206

Calligraphic merchant's diploma, Leipzig 1699.

Calligraphic page from John Clark's "Writing improv'd", London 1714.

PAGE 207

Title and ornamented page from Michael Baurenfeind's "Wiederherstellung der Schreibkünst", printed by Christoph Weigel, Nuremberg 1716.

PAGES 208–209

Calligraphic scrolls from Mánoel Andrade de Figueiredo's "Nova Escola", Lisboa 1722.

PAGE 210

Ornamented page from Johann Georg Schwandner's "Disertatio de Calligraphia", Vienna 1756.

PAGE 211

Ornamented pages from Johann Merken's "Liber artificiosus Alphabeti majoris", Mühlheim 1782.

PAGE 212

Title page from Joaquim José Ventura da Silva's "Regas Methodicas", Lisboa 1803.

Calligraphic scroll by Johann Evangelist Mettenleiter, Munich 1850.

PAGE 213

Calligraphic title from a Hebrew manuscript, Germany 10th century.

Calligraphic title from a Hebrew manuscript, Cologne 1571.

PAGE 214

Kufic-Arabic leaf from the Koran, Mesopotamia 7th century.

Kufic-Arabic leaf from the Koran, Mesopotamia 9th century.

PAGE 215

Arabic leaf from the Koran, North Africa 15th century.

Calligraphic proverb (Bismillah), Persia 17th century.

PAGE 216

Calligraphic signature (Bismillah) of Beha Ullah, Emir of the Babi tribe, Persia.

Calligraphic signature (Thugra) of Sulaiman I the Magnificent, Turkey 1520–1566.

PAGE 217

Calligraphic rosace at the mosque of Sulaiman I the Magnificent, Constantinople 16th century.

Moorish-Arabic inscription at the Alhambra, Granada 13th century.

PAGE 218

Calligraphic inscription by Emperor T'ai-Tsung, China 970–998.

SCRIPT AND SCROLLS

THE ART of occidental and oriental writing has been thoroughly studied and ably presented by past and contemporary experts and scholars in their many excellent books and papers on the development of lettering. In nearly every one of these books and treatises, the composition and assessment of the material presented is based strictly on a calligraphic point of view. The main stress of these searching and scholarly papers is on the derivation and evolution of the letter and the alphabet.

It is unfortunate for the interested artist who is not an inveterate lettering man, that the ornamental expressions of the old writing-masters in title pages, borders and flourishes, found in abundance in their sample books and other works, are passed over or brushed aside as unimportant and unnecessary frills in most of these dissertations. Scrolls and calligraphic figure drawings are condemned altogether as ugly degenerations of the art of writing.

The ornamented compositions of the old writing-masters who were inspired by the art of the oriental miniaturist-calligraphers have a decorative value of their own. They show not only the high skill of these craftsmen, but also their artistic realization of the use of calligraphic expressions in design.

From a decorative point of view these scrolls and flourishes are a treasure chest of ornamental gems and a well of delight for the artist, the craftsman and the amateur.

Calligraphic letter E/GERMANY 15TH CENTURY

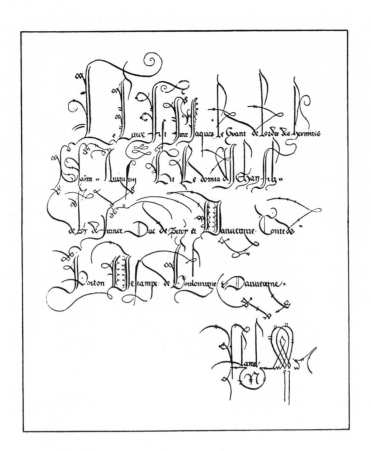

Calligraphic book plates by Nicolas Flamel / PARIS 14TH CENTURY

Ad vsum celeberrime ecclesie Eboracensis.

*Ornamented title printed by M. P. Oliveri/*ROUEN 1490

*Calligraphic title printed by Wynkyn de Worde/*LONDON 1495

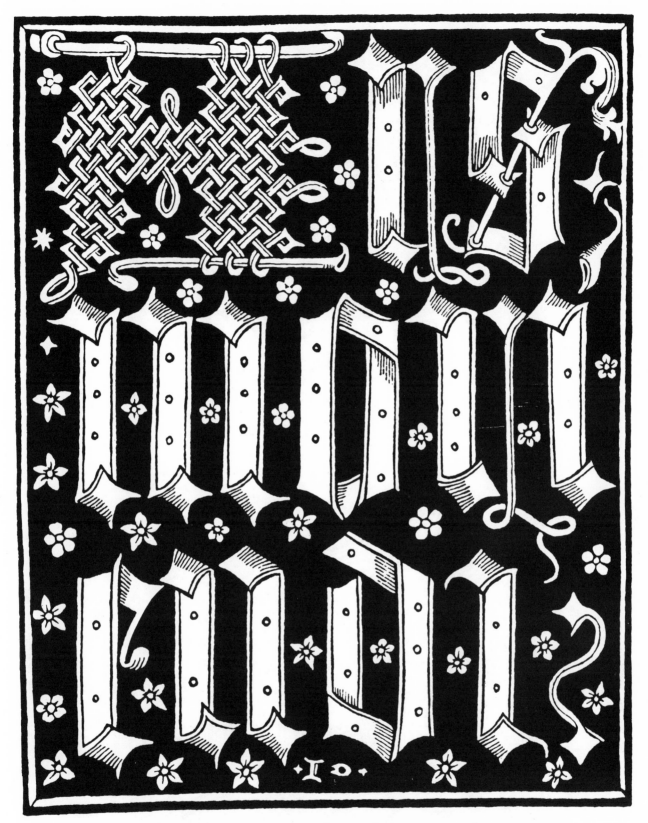

Cum orationibus pulcherrimis dicendis circa agonizantem.

Ornamented title page designed by Jean Duvet / LYONS 1496

Calligraphic title printed by Anton Koberger / NUREMBERG 1498

Calligraphic title printed by Iaccuinus de Tridino / VENICE 1502

Ornamented title printed by Richard Pynson/LONDON 1515

Calligraphic title printed by Johannes Taccuinus/VENICE 1517

Calligraphic title by Melchior Lotter / WITTENBERG 1522

Calligraphic page by Nicolaus Werner / GERMANY 16TH CENTURY

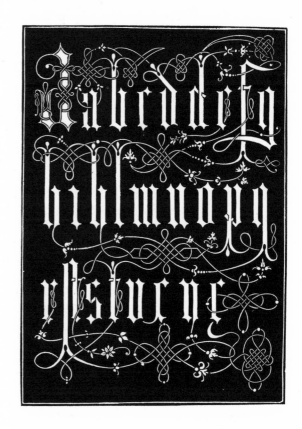

Ornamented pages by Giovanni Antonio Tagliente / VENICE 1524

Chronica ·

des gantzen · Teütsch=

en lands / aller Teütschen völ=

cker herkomen / Namen / Händeln / Güten vñ bösen
Thaten / Reden / Rhäten / Kriegen / Sigen / Niderlagen / Stifftungen.
Veränderungen der Sitze / Reich / Länder / Religion / Gesatze / Polocey /
Spraach / völcker vnd sitten / Vor vñ nach Christi geburt / Von Noe biß
auff Carolum 5. Ankunfft vnd stifftung der Reich / Bistumb / Fürsten=
thumb / Herrschafften / Stett / Clöster vnd Stifft. Genealogia vnd Ge=
schlecht Register der Potentaten vñ Thurniers gnossen. Wie vil län=
der vnd völcker Germania begreiff / vnd wie weit jre Grentzen er=
strecke / wie offt sie inander Länder jre sitz verruckt / wie vil kü=
nigreich besetzt / vnd wie vil völcker von jn vßgangen / her=
komen. Auch von der Teütschen vralten / alten vnd
newen sitten / bräuchen vnd Pollecy. Item von
Teütscher nation geschwellen / gelegenheyt / fruchtpar=
keyt vnd eygentschafft. Auß glaubwirdigen
angenomen / Geschichtschreibern /
zů ruck diß blats ver=
zeychenet / zůsamen getragen / Vnd die Teütschen den Teütschen zů Teütsch / sich
selbs darinn / als in einem Spiegel zů ersehen / fürgestelt.
Durch Sebastian Francken /
von Wörd.

Title page printed by Mathias Apiarius / BERN 1539

Gemeiner lobli-
cher Eydgnoschafft Stetten/
Landen vnd Völckeren Chronick wir-
diger thaaten beschreybūg.

Hieriñ wirt auch die gelegenheit der gantzen
Europe/ Item ein kurtzuergriffne Chronica Germanie oder Teiitsch-
lands/in sonders aber ein fleyssige histori vnd ordenliche beschreybung Gallie oder Franck-
rychs fürgestellt/darauff deñ obgedachte der Eydgnoschafft beschreybung volget. Welchs
alles mit gar schönen Geographischen Landtaflen/ Contrafettschem abmalen der Stetten/
Fläcken vnd Schlachten/auch mit vilen alten vnd herrlichen Waapen/künigklicher/
fürstlicher vnd Edler geschlächten oder Geburtstaflen fürgebildet/darzū mit
fleyssigen Registern aufgescheiden/Durch Johann Stumpffen beschū
ben/vnd in XIII. bücher abgeteilt ist. Welcher summen vnd
inhalt nach 5.náchst vmbgewendten blettern
eigentlich verzeichnet findst.

M· D·   XLVIII·

Getruckt Zürych in der Eydgnoschafft
bey Christoffel Froschouer.

Title page printed by Christoph Froschauer / ZURICH 1548

THESAVRARIVM
ARTIS SCRIPTORIAE ET

cancellariæ Scribarumq3 Clenodium pretiosum Libellus plane au-
reus varia ex vero deprompta fudamento scripta continens
antea non visa
nuc primum in lucem ædita
CASPARE NEVIO COLONIÆ AGRIP-
pinæ Scriba & Arithmetico authore Anno redep toris nostri
1 5 4 9.

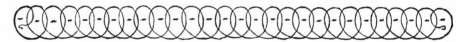

Scripta hoc in Thesaurario contesa sunt Latina Italica
Gallica Germanica Brabatica & Anglica

Vbioq3 um Coloniæ Agrippinæ cælasum & impressum Impensis
Casparis Vopelij Medeb. Mathematum professoris
cum Gratia & priuilegio Cæsariæ Maiestatis ad decennium

Title page and frontispiece by Caspar Neff / COLOGNE 1549

Calligraphic lettering by Caspar Neff / COLOGNE 1549

Calligraphic broadside / NUREMBERG 1571

Title page by Jacob Jacobelln / STRASBOURG 1579

Ornamented page from a manuscript / GERMANY 16TH CENTURY

Calligraphic pages by Jan van den Velde / ROTTERDAM 1605

Calligraphic page by De Beaugrand / PARIS 1601

Calligraphic title page by Maria Strick / DELFT 1607

Ornamented pages by Salomon Henrix and Petrus Bales / AMSTERDAM 1614

Calligraphic title page by Richard Gething/LONDON 1619

Calligraphic page by Periccioli/SIENA 1619

Scrolls by Geobattista Pisani/GENOA 1640

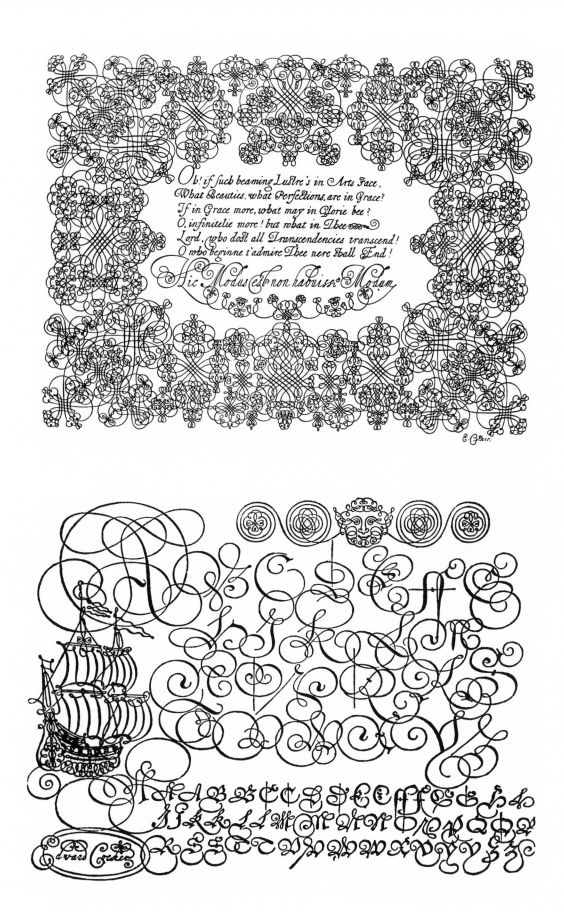

Scrolls by Edward Cocker / LONDON 1657

Scrolls by Edward Cocker / LONDON 1661 AND 1672

The
Pen-mans Paradis:
both Pleaſant & Profitable
OR
Examples of all ẙ usuall Hands of this Kingdome
Adorn'd with variety of ſſigures and Flouriſhes done by
Command of Hand. Each ſſigure being one continued &
entire Tract of the Pen most whereof may be struck as
well Reverse (or to answer both wayes) as Forward. &c.
Invented and Perform'd
John Seddon

Sold by Wᵐ Court at ẙ Mariner & Anchor on little Tower hill London

Blind Fortune favours still blind ignorance
And her unworthy Offspring doth advance
Whilst wiſe men ſeldome meet a lucky chance.
Seddon

Scrolls by John Seddon / LONDON 1695

Calligraphic merchants' diploma / LEIPZIG 1699

Calligraphic page by John Clark / LONDON 1714

Ornamented pages by Michael Baurenfeind / NUREMBERG 1716

Scroll by Mánoel Andrade de Figueiredo/LISBON 1722

Igualmente ordenou Deos o fiemamento do Ceo, que o desua Igreja: no do Ceo collocou o Sol, que presidisse ao dia, ea Lua à noite: no desua Igreja constituio ao Summo Pontifice Sol, que goveenasse a Luz do espirito; e ao Principe Catholico Lua que regesse as sombras do goveeno temporal.

Andrade.

Scroll by Mánoel Andrade de Figueiredo / LISBON 1722

Ornamented page by Johann Georg Schwandner/VIENNA 1756

Ornamented pages by Johann Merken/MÜHLHEIM 1782

Scroll by Joaquin José Ventura da Silva / LISBON 1803

Scroll by Johann Evangelist Mettenleiter / MUNICH 1850

Hebrew title from a manuscript/GERMANY 10TH CENTURY

Hebrew title from a manuscript/COLOGNE 1571

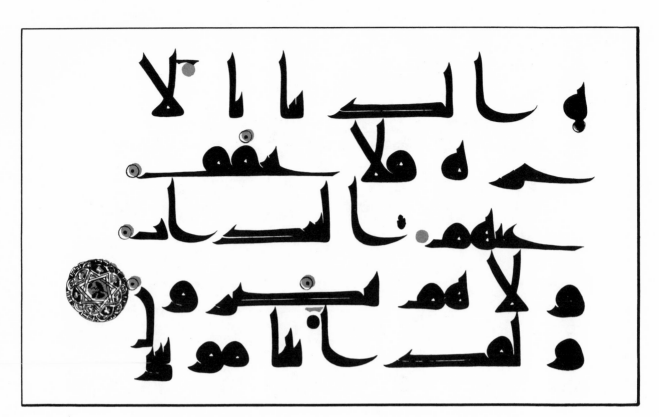

Kufic-Arabic leaf from the Koran / MESOPOTAMIA 7TH CENTURY

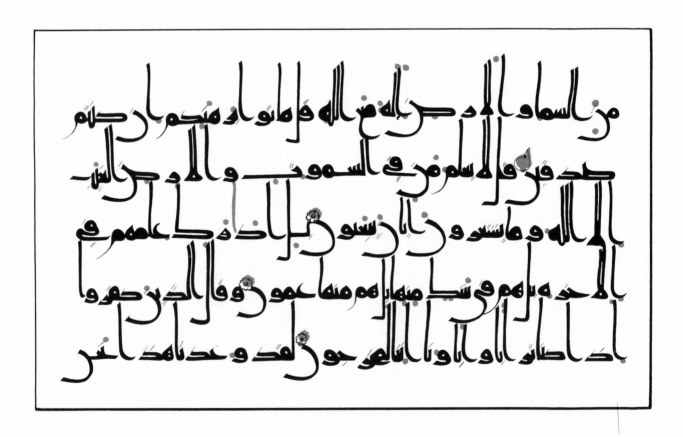

Kufic-Arabic leaf from the Koran / MESOPOTAMIA 9TH CENTURY

Arabic leaf from the Koran / NORTH AFRICA 15TH CENTURY

Calligraphic proverb (Bismillah) / PERSIA 17TH CENTURY

*Calligraphic signature (Bismillah) of Emir Beha Ullah/*PERSIA

*Signature (Thugra) of Sulaiman I the Magnificent/*TURKEY 1520–1566

Rosace from the mosque of Sulaiman I / CONSTANTINOPLE 16TH CENTURY

Arabic inscription from the Alhambra / GRANADA 13TH CENTURY

義靜三藏於西天取得此
梵書唵字所在之處一切
鬼神見聞無不驚怖
太宗皇帝讚
鶴立蚍行勢未休五天文
字鬼神愁儒門弟子無人
識穿耳胡僧笑點頭

Calligraphic inscription by Emperor T'ai-Tsung/CHINA 970–998

·218·

HERALDIC ORNAMENTS &
ALLEGORIC CARTOUCHES

Seal of Edward the Confessor/ENGLAND 1043–1066

HERALDIC ORNAMENTS AND ALLEGORIC
CARTOUCHES

PAGE 219
Seal of Edward the Confessor, King of the English, 1042–1066.

PAGE 221
Calligraphic sigil of Alfonso X the Wise, King of Castille and Leon, 1226–1284.

PAGE 222
Seal of Rudolf I of Hapsburg, Holy Roman Emperor, 1273–1291.

PAGE 223
Seal and counter seal of Margaret of France, second Queen of Edward I of England, 1299.

Seal and counter seal of Thomas De Beauchamp, III Earl of Warwick, 1369.

Seal of John Holland, Earl of Huntington, Lord Admiral of England, 1436.

Seal of Sir Robert Hungerford, 1449.

PAGE 224
Tree of affinity from Henricus Bartolomaei de Segusio's "Summa Super Titulis Decretalium", printed by Ludwig Hohenwang, Augsburg 1477.

Tree of affinity from Crispus Joannes de Montibus' "Repetitio tituli de Heredibus", printed by Joannes Hamman De Landoia, Venice 1490.

PAGE 225
Pedigree of Leopold zu Babenberg from Ladislas Suntheim's "Der löblichen Fürsten un des Lands Österrich altharkome un Regierung", printed by Michael Furter, Basel 1491.

PAGE 226
Family diagram of Albrecht von Sachsen from "Chroneken der Sassen", printed by Peter Schöffer, Mainz 1492.

Tree of succession of the saints of the Carthus Order from "Vita B. Brunonsis", printed by Johann Bergmann, Basel 1499.

Tree of succession (St. Dominicus), France 15th century.

PAGE 227
Heraldic title page from Robertus Ganguinus' "De origine et gestis Francorum", printed by Thielmann Kerver, Paris 1500.

PAGE 228
Religious diagrams (St. Bonaventure) from "Opuscula", printed by Jacob de Leucho, Venice 1504.

Religious diagram (St. Franciscus) from "Liber Conformitatum", printed by Gotardo da Ponte, Venice 1510.

PAGE 229
Heraldic title page from Diego de Gumiel's "Aureum Opus", Valencia 1515.

PAGE 230
Heraldic title page from "Reformacion der Baÿrischn Lanndrecht", designed by Casper Clofigl, printed by Johann Schobsser, Munich 1518.

PAGE 231
Albrecht Dürer's "Emperor Maximilian I", Nuremberg 1519.

PAGES 232–233
Pedigree of Emperor Maximilian I from Albrecht Dürer's "Triumphal Arch", Nuremberg 1515–1519.

PAGE 234
The great seal and counter seal of England, 1527.

Cartouches from "Grammatices Rudimenta", printed by Donato Aelio, Venice 1532.

PAGE 235
Family tree of Ferdinand of Austria, printed by Robert Peril, Amsterdam 1540.

Cartouche "St. Sebaldus", Nuremberg 1540.

PAGE 236
Map cartouche from Lafreri's "Britannae Insulae", Rome 1546.

Religious diagram (Bonifacius VIII) from Aegidi Perrini's "Sextus Deretalium Liber", printed by Hugo à Porta, Lyons 1559.

PAGE 237
Allegoric title page from Romulus Amasaeus' "Pavsaniae Veteris Graeciae Descriptio", printed by Lorenzo Torrentino, Florence 1551.

PAGE 238
Heraldic title page from "Erklärung der Landsfreihait", Ingolstadt 1553.

PAGE 239

Allegoric title page from Matheus Merian's "Topographia Galliae", printed by Caspar Merian, Basel 1555.

PAGE 240

Map cartouches from Abraham Ortelius' "Theatrum orbis terrarum", Antwerp 1570–1584.

PAGE 241

Pedigree of King Henry VIII from Geoffrey Chaucer's "The Caunterburie tales", London 1561.

PAGE 242

Cartouches by F. de Wit, Antwerp 1568.

Sigil of the University of Oxford, 16th century.

Seal and counter seal of the Kings Council, Colony of Virginia 1606.

PAGE 243

Book stamp of Jacopo Bocompagni, Duke of Sora, 1612.

Book stamp of John Williams, Bishop of Lincoln, afterwards Archbishop of York, 1642–1650.

Sigil of Peter Stuyvesant, Governor of New Netherland, 1647–1664.

Seal and counter seal of King William III and Queen Mary of England, 1689–1695.

PAGE 244

Cartouches from Italian maps, 17th century.

PAGE 245

Sigil of the Printers Guild, Jena 1720.

Diagram of the Printers Guild, Regensburg 1740.

PAGE 246

Book stamp of Baptist Noel, III Earl of Gainsborough, 1714.

Book stamp of Hugh Boscawen, Viscount Falmouth, 1715.

Book stamp of Pope Pius VI, 1775–1799.

Calligraphic sigil of Alfonso the Wise/SPAIN 1226–1284

HERALDIC ORNAMENTS AND
ALLEGORIC CARTOUCHES

HERALDIC ORNAMENTS and allegoric decorations are the most extensive and elaborate single groups in applied art. The use of seals and cartouches is as old as Egypt, Babylonia and Assyria. Allegoric designs were already employed in early Greek, Etruscan and Roman mythologic art. You could fill to overflowing voluminous libraries and collections with the uncountable legions of medieval seals, stamps, family trees, pedigrees, religious diagrams, worldly and ecclesiastical adornments, title pages of anniversary and festival pamphlets, genealogic and heraldic manuals, cartographic decorations in books on voyages and discoveries, ornaments and cartouches for maps and atlases.

Their inestimable number, their unrestrained galaxy in forms and shapes, their overwhelming abundance in simple and elaborate decorative elements are an inexhaustible mine of inspiration for every designer and craftsman.

Seals and stamps in their old heraldic forms and applications are still part of our everyday life. They are used to establish the right of private ownership, to confirm the authenticity of documents and signatures, and to underline the position of certain office holders.

Pedigrees and trees are finding an extensive variety of uses in the more commercialized form of graphs and diagrams in today's science, technique, economy, commerce, administration and communication.

Figurative and embellished charts and maps are designed in abundance today by leading contemporary artists for wall decorations and illustrations. Cartouches are also widely used for trade marks, labels and advertisements.

Seal of Rudolf I of Hapsburg, Holy Roman Emperor / 1273–1291

Seal of Margaret of France / 1299

Seal of Thomas De Beauchamp / 1369

Seal of John Holland / 1436   *Seal of Robert De Hungerford / 1449*

Tree of affinity printed by Ludwig Hohenwang / AUGSBURG 1477

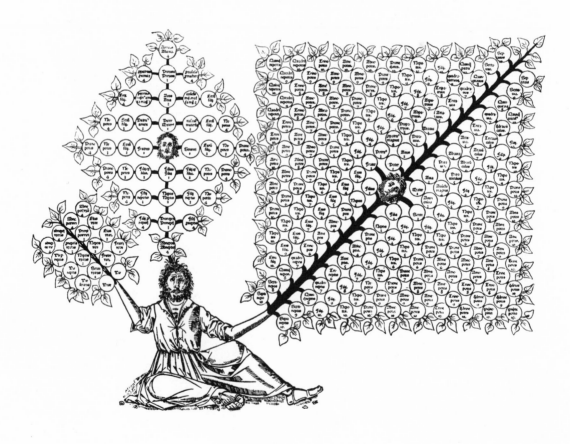

Tree of affinity printed by Joannes Hamman de Landoia / VENICE 1490

Leopold Margraff In österreich vnd graff zu Babenberg

Pedigree of Leopold zu Babenberg/BASEL 1491

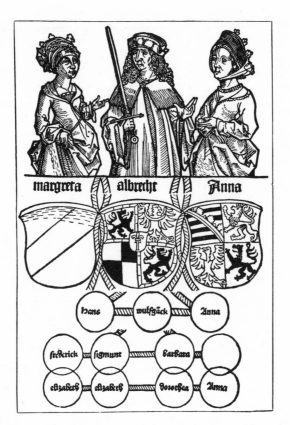

Family diagram of Albrecht von Sachsen / MAINZ 1492

Tree of succession / BASEL 1499

Tree of succession / FRANCE 15TH CENTURY

Heraldic title page printed by Thielmann Kerver / PARIS 1500

· 227 ·

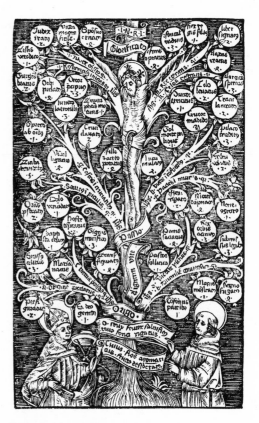

Religious diagrams by Jacob de Leucho / VENICE 1504

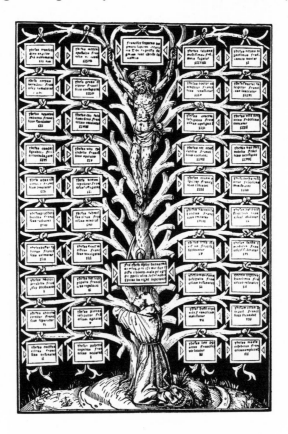

Religious diagram by Gotardo da Ponte / VENICE 1510

Areum opus regalium priuilegiorum ciuita
tis et regni Ualentie cum historia cristianissi
mi Regis Jacobi ipsius primi aquistatoris

Heraldic title page printed by Diego de Gumiel / VALENCIA 1515

Reformacion der bayrischn lanndrecht nach Cristj vnsers Hailmachers geburde Im fünftzehenhundert vnnd Achtzehendm jar aufgericht-

Heraldic title page by Casper Clofigl / MUNICH 1518

IMPERATOR
DIVVS MAXI
PIVSFELIX

CAESAR
MILIANVS
AVGVSTVS·

Emperor Maximilian I by Albrecht Dürer / NUREMBERG 1519

Pedigree of Maximilian I by Albrecht Dürer/NUREMBERG 1515–1519

Pedigree of Maximilian I by Albrecht Dürer / NUREMBERG 1515–1519

The great seal and counter seal / ENGLAND 1527

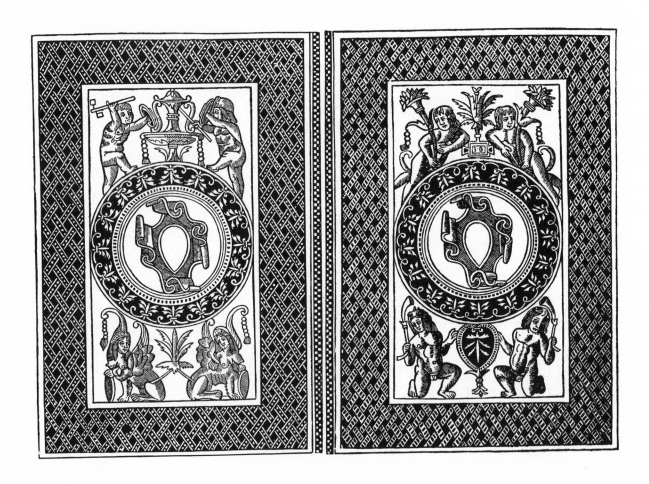

Cartouches by Donato Aelio / VENICE 1532

Family tree of Ferdinand of Austria by Robert Peril/AMSTERDAM 1540

Cartouche "Saint Sebaldus"/NUREMBERG 1540

Map cartouche by Lafreri/ROME 1546

Religious diagram by Hugo à Porta/LYONS 1559

Allegoric title page printed by Lorenzo Torrentino / FLORENCE 1551

Heraldic title page/INGOLSTADT 1553

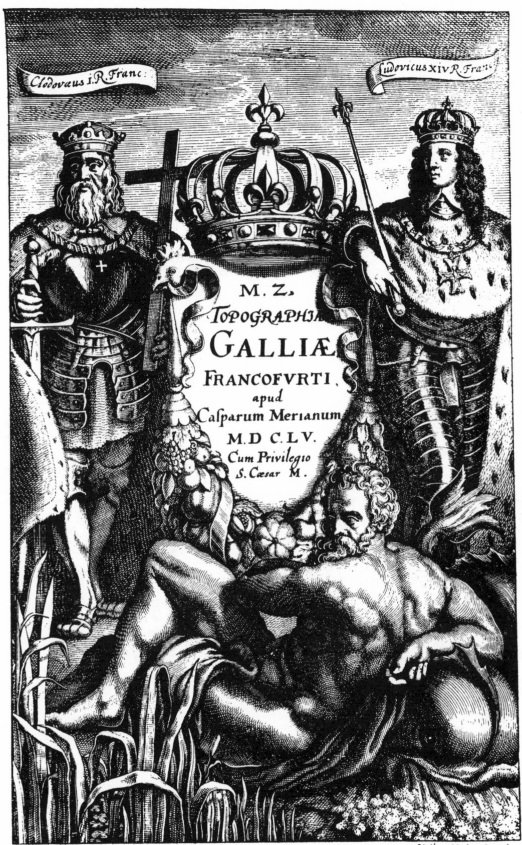

Allegoric title page by Matheus Merian/BASEL 1555

TAR
TARIAE
SIVE MAG
NI CHAMI
REGNI
typus

BVRGVN
DIAE IN
FERIORIS,
QVÆ DVCA
TVS NOMI
NE CENSE
TVR, DES.
1584.

CVM PRIVILEGIO IM
PERIALI ET BELGICO
AD DECENNIVM

BAVARIAE,
OLIM VIN
DELICIAE,
DELINEATI
ONIS COM
PENDIVM
*Ex tabula Philippi
Apiani Math.*

Map cartouches by Abraham Ortelius / ANTWERP 1570–1584

Pedigree of King Henry VIII / LONDON 1561

Cartouches by F. de Wit / ANTWERP 1568

Sigil of the University of Oxford / 16TH CENTURY

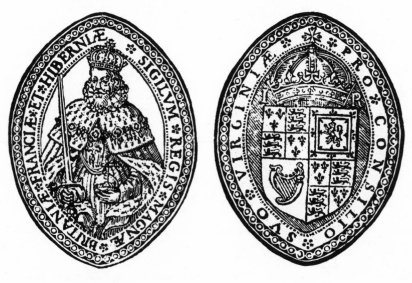

Seal and counter seal of the Kings Council / COLONY OF VIRGINIA 1606

Book stamp of Jacopo Bocampagni,
Duke of Sora / 1612

Book stamp of John Williams,
Bishop of Lincoln / 1642–1650

Sigil of Governor Peter Stuyvesant / NEW NETHERLAND 1647–1664

The great seal of King William III and Queen Mary / ENGLAND 1689–1695

Map cartouches / ITALY 17TH CENTURY

Sigil of the Printers Guild / JENA 1720

Diagram of the Printers Guild / REGENSBURG 1740

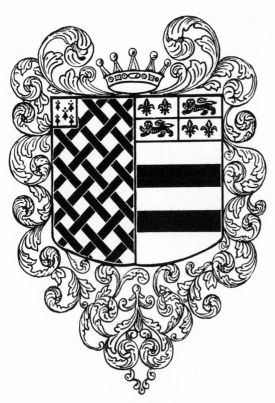

Book stamp of Baptist Noel,
Earl of Gainsborough/1714

Book stamp of Hugh Boscawen,
Viscount Falmouth/1715

Book stamp of Pope Pius VI/ROME 1775–1799

BIBLIOGRAPHY

The K. K. Garellian Public Library at the Theresiano in Vienna/1780

BIBLIOGRAPHY

[The works indicated by an asterisk have been reprinted by Dover Publications.]

PRINTING AND TYPOGRAPHY

ALVIN, M. *Les Commencements de la gravure aux Pays-Bas.* Bruxelles, 1857.

AMES, JOSEPH. *Typographical antiquities or the history of printing in England, Scotland and Ireland.* London, 1810–1819, W. Miller.

ANDREÄISCHE BUCHHANDLUNG. *Probeblätter.* Frankfurt a.M., 1838.

AUDIN, MARIUS. *Histoire de l'Imprimerie.* Paris, 1929, Henri Jonquières.

———. *Le livre, son illustration, sa décoration.* Paris, 1926, C. Crès & Cie.

———. *Les livrets typographiques des fonderies françaises créées avant 1800.* Paris, 1933, Pégasus.

AUER, ALOIS. *Typenschau des gesammten Erdkreises.* Wien, 1844, Hof- & Staatsdruckerei.

BAUER, KONRAD F. *Aventur und Kunst.* Frankfurt a.M., 1940, Bauersche Giesserei.

*BEARDSLEY, AUBREY VINCENT. *The early and the later work of . . .* London, 1899–1912, John Lane.

BEYERHAUS, A. *Schriftproben.* Berlin, 1840.

BLADES, WILLIAM. *The Pentateuch of Printing.* Chicago, 1891, McClurg & Co.

BLISS, DOUGLAS PERCY. *A History of Wood Engraving.* London, 1928, Dent & Sons.

BODONI, GIAMBATTISTA. *Manuale Tipografico.* Parma, 1818.

BROWN, HORATIO (ROBERT FORBES). *The Venetian Printing Press.* New York, 1891, G. P. Putnam's Sons.

BRUN, (HENRI) MARCELIN AIMÉ. *Manuel pratique de la Typographie Française.* Paris, 1825, Firmin Didot.

BÜCHLER, EDWARD. *Die Anfänge des Buchdruckes in der Schweiz.* Bern, 1930, Schweizerisches Gutenbergmuseum Bibl. No. 2.

CHATTO, WILLIAM ANDREW. *A Treatise of Wood-Engraving.* London, 1839, Knight & Co.

CLAUDIN, ANATOLE. *Histoire de l'Imprimerie en France au XVe et XVIe Siècle.* Paris, 1900–1914, Imprimerie Nationale.

CONWAY, W. C. *The woodcutters of the Netherlands in the 15th century.* Cambridge, 1884.

CRANE, WALTER. *The decorative illustration of books.* London, 1896, G. Bell & Sons.

DENIS, MICHAEL. *Die Merkwürdigkeiten der k.k.garellischen öffentlichen Bibliothek am Thersiano.* Wien, 1780, Augustin Bernardi.

DE VINNE, THEODORE LOW. *The Invention of Printing.* New York, 1876, Francis Hart & Co.

———. *Titlepages as seen by a printer.* New York, 1901, Grolier Club.

DIDOT, AMBROISE FIRMIN. *Catalogue illustré des dessins et estampes.* Paris, 1877.

———. *Essai typographique et bibliographique de l'histoire de la gravure sur bois.* Paris, 1863.

DODGSON, CAMPBELL. *Catalogue of Early German and Flemish Woodcuts in the British Museum.* London, 1903–1911, Longmans & Co.

DUFF, EDWARD GORDON. *Early English Printing.* London, 1896, Kegan Paul, Trench, Trübner & Co.

DUPORTAL, JEANNE. *Études sur les livres a figures édités en France de 1601–1660.* Paris, 1914, Honoré Champion.

ENGEL, JOHANN JOSEPH. *Specimen Characterum Latinorum, Hungaricorum et Bosniaco-Croaticorum.* Pecs-Fünfkirchen, 1773.

ENSCHEDÉ, ADRIAN JUSTUS. *Spécimen de caractères typographiques anciens.* Haarlem, 1867, J. Enschedé en Zonen.

ENSCHEDÉ, CHARLES. *Fonderies de caractères et leur matériel dans les Pays-Bas du XVe au XIXe siècle.* Haarlem, 1908, De Erven F. Bohn.

ENSCHEDÉ, J. *Proof van Letteren.* Haarlem, 1768.

ERNESTI, JOHANN HEINRICH GOTTFRIED. *Die Wol-eingerichtete Buchdruckerey.* Nürnberg, 1721, Johann Andrea Endters Erben.

ESTEVES DOS SANTOS, RAUL. *A arte negra.* Lisboa, 1941, Editorial Império.

FAGAN, LOUIS. *History of engraving in England.* London, 1893.

FALKENSTEIN, KARL CONSTANTIN. *Geschichte der Buchdruckerkunst in ihrer Entstehung und Ausbildung.* Leipzig, 1840, B. G. Teubner.

FARMER, LITTLE & Co. *Specimen book of printing Types.* New York, 1862.

———. *Specimens of printing Types, Ornaments and Borders.* New York, 1873.

FAULMANN, KARL. *Illustrierte Geschichte der Buchdruckerkunst.* Wien, 1882, A. Hartleben.

FOURNIER, JR., PIERRE-SIMON. *Manuel Typographique.* Paris, 1764–1766, J. Barbou.

———. *Modéles des Caractères de l'Imprimerie.* Paris, 1742.

FRÄNGLER, WILHELM. *Altdeutsches Bilderbuch.* Leipzig, 1930, H. Stubenrauch.

FRIEDLÄNDER, MAX J. *Holzschnitte von Hans Weiditz.* Berlin, 1922, Verein f. Kunstwissenschaften.

GERLACH, MARTIN. *Das alte Buch und seine Ausstattung.* Wien-Leipzig, 1915, Die Quelle No. 13.

GILLÉ, JOSEPH. *Épreuves des Caractères.* Paris, 1773.

GOETZE, ALFRED AUGUST WOLDEMAR. *Die hochdeutschen Drucker der Reformationszeit.* Strassburg, 1905, Karl J. Trübner.

GOLLOB, HEDWIG. *Der Wiener Holzschnitt von 1490–1550.* Wien, 1926, Krystal Verlag.

GRAUTOFF, OTTO. *Moderne Buchkunst in Deutschland.* Leipzig, 1901, Hermann Seemann Nachf.

GRESS, EDMUND GEIGER. *The Art and Practise of Typography.* New York, 1910, Oswald Publishing Co.

GRÜNBERG, JEANNOT. *Iwan Fedorow.* Leipzig, 1911, Archiv für Buchgewerbe.

GUTENBERG FESTSCHRIFT. Mainz, 1925, Gutenberg Gesellschaft.

HAEBLER, KONRAD. *Der Deutsche Drucker des XV.Jahrhunderts im Auslande.* München, 1924, Jacques Rosenthal.

———. *Geschichte der spanischen Frühdrucke in Stammbäumen.* Leipzig, 1923, K. W. Hiersemann.

———. *Der italienische Wiegendruck in Original-Typenbeispielen.* München, 1927, Weiss & Co.

HAUSENSTEIN, WILHELM. *Rokoko.* München, 1924, R. Piper & Co.

HECKETHORN, CHARLES WILLIAM. *The Printers of Basle in the XV and XVI Centuries.* London, 1897, Unwin Bros.

HEITZ, PAUL. *Originalabdrücke von Formschneiderarbeiten des XVI., XVII. und XVIII. Jahrhunderts.* Strassburg, 1892–1899, Heitz & Mündel.

HELLER, JOSEPH. *Geschichte der Holzschneidekunst.* Bamberg, 1823, C. F. Kunz.

*HIND, ARTHUR MAYGER. *A history of engraving and etching.* London, 1908, Constable & Co.

* ———. *A history of woodcut.* London, 1935, Constable & Co.

HIRTH, GEORGE and MUTHER, RICHARD. *Meisterholzschnitte aus vier Jahrhunderten.* München, 1893.

HOLTROP, JAN WILLEM. *Monuments typographiques des Pays-Bas.* La Haye, 1868, M. Nijhoff.

HUMPHREYS, HENRY NOEL. *A History of the Art of Printing.* London, 1867, Bernard Quaritch.

IMPRIMERIE NATIONALE. *Specimen des caractères, vignettes, armes, trophées et fleurons de l'Imprimerie Royale.* Paris, 1819.

JANSEN, HENRIK. *Essai sur l'Origine de la Gravure en Bois et en Taille-douce.* Paris, 1808, F. Schoell.

JOHNSON, ALFRED FORBES. *One hundred Titlepages 1500–1800.* London, 1928, John Lane.

KAPPENS, JOHANN ERHARD. *Die so nöthige und nützliche Buchdruckerkunst und Schriftgiesserey.* Leipzig, 1740–1745, Christian Friedrich Gessner.

KEHRLI, J. OTTO. *Typographie und Kunst.* Bern, 1945, Schweizerisches Gutenbergmuseum.

KRISTELLER, PAUL. *Early Florentine Woodcuts.* London, 1897, Kegan Paul, Trench, Trübner & Co.

———. *Kupferstich und Holzschnitt in vier Jahrhunderten.* Berlin, 1922, Bruno Cassierer.

———. *Die Lombardische Graphik der Renaissance.* Berlin, 1913, Bruno Cassierer.

*KURTH, WILLI. *Albrecht Dürers sämtliche Holzschnitte.* München, 1927, Holbein Verlag.

KUTSCHMANN, TH. *Geschichte der deutschen Illustration.* Goslar, 1899, F. Jäger.

LABITTE, ADOLPHE. *Gravure sur bois tirées des livres français du XVe siècle.* Paris, 1868.

LACROIX, PAUL and FOURNIER, EDUARD. *Histoire de l'imprimerie et des arts et professions.* Paris, 1852, Ferdinand Seré.

LEJARD, ANDRÉ. *The art of the French Book.* Paris, 1947, Du Chêne.

LIPPMANN, FRIEDRICH. *Italian Wood engravings in the Fifteenth Century.* London, 1888, Bernard Quaritch.

——— and DOHME, R. *Druckschriften des XV.bis XVIII.Jahrhunderts in getreuen Nachbildungen.* Berlin, 1884–1887, Reichsdruckerei.

LOUISY, M. P. *Le Livre et les Arts qui s'y rattachent.* Paris, 1887, Firmin Didot.

LOYSON & BRIQUET. *Épreuve des Caractères.* Paris, 1751.

LUCE, LOUIS RENÉ. *Épreuve du premier alphabet droit et penché, ornée de quadres et de cartouches.* Paris, 1740, Imprimerie Royale.

———. *Essai d'une Nouvelle Typographie.* Paris, 1771, J. Barbou.

LUCKOMBE, PHILIP. *The History and Art of Printing.* London, 1771, J. Johnson.

LÜTZOW, C. VON. *Geschichte des deutschen Kupferstichs und Holzschnitts.* Berlin, 1891.

MACKELLAR, SMITH & JORDAN. *Specimens of Printing Types.* Philadelphia, 1873.

MCMURTRIE, DOUGLAS CRAWFORD. *The golden book.* Chicago, 1927, Pascal Covici.

MANTEUFFEL, K. ZOEGE VON. *Der deutsche Kupferstich.* München, 1922, Hugo Schmidt.

MARTIN, HENRY MARIE RADEGONDE. *Le Livre Français des Origines à la fin du Second Empire.* Paris-Bruxelles, 1924, G. van Oest.

MASSÉNA, VICTOR (PRINCE DE ESSLING). *Les livres à figures vénetiens de la fin du XVe siècle et du commencement du XVIe.* Paris, 1889–1890, Henri Leclerc.

MAYER, ANTON. *Wiens Buchdruckergeschichte.* Wien, 1883–1887, W. Frick.

MEYNELL, SIR FRANCIS. *English printed books.* London, 1946, Collins.

——— and MORISON, STANLEY. *Causerie numero neuf où l'on parle du fleuron en typographie.* London, 192?.

MORISON, STANLEY. *The Art of the Printer.* London, 1925, Ernest Benn.

———. *Four centuries of fine printing.* New York, 1949, Farrar & Straus.

——— and JACKSON, HOLBROOK. *A brief survey of printing history and practice.* London, 1923, The Fleuron.

MUTHER, RICHARD. *Die deutsche Buchillustration der Gothik und Frührenaissance.* München, 1884, George Hirth.

NIJHOFF, WOUTER. *L'art typographique dans les Pays-Bas.* La Haye, 1926.

ONGANIA, FERDINANDO. *L'arte della stampa nel rinascimento italiano.* Venezia, 1894.

———. *Early Venetian Printing.* Venezia, 1895.

PAPILLON, JEAN BAPTISTE MICHEL. *Traité historique et pratique de la gravure de bois.* Paris, 1766, P. G. Simon.

PFLUGK-HARTUNG, JULIUS ALBERT GEORG VON. *Rahmen deutscher Buchtitel im XVI. Jahrhundert.* Stuttgart, 1909, Fritz Lehmann.

PHILIPPE, JULES PIERRE JOSEPH. *Origine de l'Imprimerie à Paris.* Paris, 1885, Charavay Frères.

POLLARD, ALFRED WILLIAM. *Early illustrated books.* London, 1893, Kegan Paul, Trench, Trübner & Co.

———. *Fine Books.* London, 1912, The Connoisseur.

REDGRAVE, GILBERT RICHARD. *Erhard Ratdolt and his work at Venice.* London, 1894, Bibliographical Society Monograph No. 1.

REED, TALBOT BAINES. *A History of the Old English Letter Foundries.* London, 1887, Elliot Stock.

REICHSDRUCKEREI. *Alphabete und Schriftzeichen des Morgen- und Abendlandes.* Berlin, 1924.

———. *Druckschriften des 15. bis 18. Jahrhunderts.* Berlin, 1884–1887.

———. *Randeinfassungen, Initialen und Zierleisten für den Buchdruck.* Berlin, 1884–1888.

REINER, IMRE. *Modern and Historical Typography.* St. Gallen, 1944–1950, Zollikofer & Co.

REMIZOV, ALEKSEI MICHAILOVICH. *Ivan Fedorov.* Paris, 1935, Papyrus.

RENOUVIER, JULES. *Histoire de la gravure dans les Pays-Bas.* Bruxelles, 1860.

RINGWALT, J. LUTHER. *American Encyclopaedia of Printing.* Philadelphia, 1871, J. B. Lippincott & Co.

RITCHEL VON HARTENBACH, JR., J. *Proben der Polytypen.* Erfurt, 1836.

SCHMIDT, R. W. *Die Technik in der Kunst.* Stuttgart, 1922, Dieck & Co.

SCHOEPFLIN, JOHANN DANIEL. *Vindiciae Typographicae.* Strassburg, 1760, Johann Gottfried Bauer.

SCHOTTENLOHER, KARL. *Das alte Buch.* Berlin, 1919, Schmidt & Co.

SCHRAMM, A. *Der Bilderschmuck der Frühdrucke.* Leipzig, 1920–1923, Deutsches Museum für Buch und Schrift.

SIMON, HOWARD. *500 Years of Art in Illustration.* Cleveland-New York, 1942, World Publishing.

STEINHAUSEN, GEORG. *Der Kaufmann in der deutschen Vergangenheit.* Leipzig, 1899, Eugen Diederichs.

STUDIO, THE. *The Art of the Book.* London, 1914.

THIBAUDEAU, F. *La Lettre d'Imprimerie.* Paris, 1921, Bureau de l'Édition.

THIBOUST, CLAUDE LOUIS. *Typographiae Excellentia.* Paris, 1754.

THOMAS, ISAIAH. *The History of Printing in America.* Boston-Worcester, 1810, Isaac Sturtevant.

———. *A Specimen of Printing Types.* Boston-Worcester, 1785.

*TORY, GEOFROY. *Champ Fleury.* Paris, 1529.

TRATTNER, JOHANN THOMAS. *Abdruck von denjenigen Röslein und Zierrathen welche sich in der K. K. Hofschriftgiesserey dermalen befinden.* Wien, 1760.

UPDIKE, DANIEL BERKELEY. *Printing Types, their history, forms and use.* Cambridge, Mass., 1922, Harvard University Press.

VALLANCE, AYMER. *The art of William Morris.* London, 1897, G. Bell & Sons.

VOULLIÉME, ERNST HERMANN. *Die deutschen Drucker des 15. Jahrhunderts.* Berlin, 1922, Reichsdruckerei.

WATSON, JAMES. *The History of the Art of Printing.* Edinburgh, 1713.

WEIGEL, THEODOR O. and ZESTERMANN, AUGUST CH. *Die Anfänge der Druckerkunst in Bild und Schrift.* Leipzig, 1866.

WEIGL, RUDOLPH. *Jost Amman.* Leipzig, 1854.

WHITE, JOHN T. *Type, Flowers and Ornaments.* New York, 1843.

WINKLE, CORNELIUS VAN. *The printer's guide.* New York, 1818.

WOLFFGER, GEORG. *New-Auffgesetztes Format-Büchlein.* Graz, 1670.

WORRINGER, WILHELM. *Die Altdeutsche Buchillustration.* München, 1921, R. Piper & Co.

WUTTKE, HEINRICH. *Geschichte der Schrift und des Schrifttums.* Leipzig, 1872, Ernst Fleischer.

CALLIGRAPHY AND LETTERS

ANDRADE DE FIGUEIREDO, MÁNOEL. *Nova escola para eprender a ler, escrever e contar.* Lisboa, 1722.

ASTLE, THOMAS. *The Origin and Progress of Writing.* London, 1803.

BAURENFEIND, MICHAEL. *Vollkommene Wieder-Herstellung der Schreib-Künst.* Nürnberg, 1716, Christoph Weigel.

BEAUGRAND, DE. *Poecilographie.* Paris, 1601.

BERGER, PHILIPPE. *Histoire de l'écriture dans l'antiquité.* Paris, 1891, Imprimerie Nationale.

BROWN, FRAN CHOUTEAU. *Letters and Lettering.* Boston, 1902, Bates & Guild.

BRY, JOHANN THEODOR and JOHANN ISRAEL DE. *Alphabeta et Characteres.* Frankfurt a.M. 1596.

BULLINGER, EDWIN WILSON. Alphabets, Monograms, Initials, Crests. New York, 1887.

CAMPOS FERREIRA LIMA, HENRIQUE DE. *Subsidio para um dicionário bio-bibliográfico dos caligrafos portugueses.* Lisboa, 1923, Biblioteca National.

CLARK, JOHN. *Writing improv'd.* London, 1714.

CLODD, EDWARD. *The Story of the Alphabet.* New York, 1900, D. Appleton & Co.

COCKER, EDWARD. *Multum in Parvo, or The Pen's Gallantry.* London, 1672.

———. *Penna Volans, or The young mans Accomplishment.* London, 1661.

———. *The Pen's Transcendencie, or fair Writing's Labyrinth.* London, 1657.

COTARELO Y MORI, EMILIO. *Diccionario biográfico y bibliográfico de caligrafos españoles.* Madrid, 1914–1916.

CRESCI, GIOVANNI FRANCESCO. *Il perfetto Scrittore.* Roma, 1569.

D'AVENNES, PRISSE. *L'Art arabe d'après les monuments du Kaire.* Paris, 1877.

DAY, LEWIS FORMAN. *Alphabets Old and New.* London, 1898, B. T. Batsford.

———. *Lettering in Ornament.* London, 1902, B. T. Batsford.

———. *Penmanship of the 16, 17 and 18 Centuries.* London, 1911, B. T. Batsford.

DEAN, HENRY. *Analytical guide to the art of penmanship.* New York, 1808, Hopkins & Bayard.

DEGERING, HERMANN. *Die Schrift.* Berlin, 1929, Ernst Wasmuth.

DELAMOTTE, FREEMAN GAGE. *The book of ornamental alphabets, ancient and medieval.* London, 1860.

DEMENGEOT, CHARLES. *Recueil complet de chiffres modernes à deux lettres.* Paris, 1864, A. Calavas.

DENIS, FERDINAND. *Histoire de l'Ornementation des Manuscrits.* Paris, 1880. E. Rouveyre.

DIRINGER, DAVID. *The Alphabet.* New York, 1948, Philosophical Library.

DRISCOLL, LUCY CATHERINE and TODA, KENJI. *Chinese Calligraphy.* Chicago, 1935, University of Chicago.

FAIRBANK, ALFRED. *A Book of Script.* Harmondsworth, 1949, Penguin No. 48.

———. *A Handwriting Manual.* Leicester, 1932, Dryad Press.

FAULMANN, KARL. *Das Buch der Schrift.* Wien, 1878, K.&K. Hof- & Staatsdruckerei.

———. *Illustrierte Geschichte der Schrift.* Wien, 1880, A. Hartleben.

FRAUBERGER, H. *Verzierte hebräische Schrift und jüdischer Buchschmuck.* Frankfurt a.M., 1909, Ges. zur Erforschung jüdischer Kunstdenkmäler.

FREIMANN, ARON. *Die hebräischen Incunabeln der Druckereien in Spanien und Portugal.* Mainz, 1925, Gutenberggesellschaft Festschrift.

———. *Thesaurus typographiae Hebraicae saeculi XV.* Berlin, 1924, Marx & Co.

GARDTHAUSEN, VIKTOR EMIL. *Das alte Monogramm.* Leipzig, 1924, K. W. Hiersemann.

GETHING, RICHARD. *Calligraphotechnia or The Art of faire writing*. London, 1619.

GRAY, NICOLETTE. *Nineteenth Century ornamented Letters and Title Pages*. London, 1938, Faber & Faber.

HEAL, SIR AMBROSE. *The English Writing Masters and their Copy Books*. London, 1931, Cambridge University Press.

HEITZ, PAUL. *Der Initialenschmuck in den elsässischen Drucken des XV. und XVI. Jahrhunderts*. Strassburg, 1894, Heitz & Mündel.

HONDIO, JUDOCO. *Theatrum artis scribendi*. Amsterdam, 1614.

HRACHOWINA, CARL. *Initialen, Alphabete und Randleisten verschiedener Kunstepochen*. Wien, 1883, Carl Graeser.

HUART, CLÉMENT. *Les Calligraphes et les Miniaturists de l'Orient Musulman*. Paris, 1908, Ernest Leroux.

HUMPHREYS, HENRY NOEL. *The origin and progress of the Art of Writing*. London, 1853.

JACOBELLN VOM NEWMARCK, JACOB. *Fundament Buch*. Strassburg, 1579, Bernhard Jobin.

JESSEN, PETER. *Meister der Schreibkunst aus drei Jahrhunderten*. Stuttgart, 1923, Julius Hoffmann.

JOHNSON, ALFRED FORBES. *Decorative initial letters*. London, 1931, Cresset Press.

JOHNSTON, EDWARD. *Writing, Illuminating and Lettering*. New York, 1906, MacMillan.

JÜDISCHE VOLKSKUNDE, JAHRBUCH FUR. Berlin, 1898–1929, Benjamin Harz.

KHEIRI, SATTAR. *Indische Miniaturen der Islamitischen Zeit*. Berlin, 1921, Orbis Pictus No. 6.

KILIAN, LUCAS. *Newes A B C Büchlein*. Augsburg, 1627.

KOCH, RUDOLF. *Klassische Schriften nach Zeichnungen von Gutenberg, Dürer, Morris, König, Hupp, Eckmann, Behrens u.a.* Dresden, 1908, Kühtmann.

KRUITWAGEN, BONAVENTURA. *Laat - Middeleeuwsche paleografica, paleotypica, liturgica, kalendalia, grammaticalia*. s'Gravenhage, 1942, M. Nijhoff.

KÜHNEL, ERNST. *Islamitische Kleinkunst*. Berlin, 1925, Schmidt & Co.

LAMPRECHT, KARL GOTTHARD. *Initialornamentik des 8. bis 13. Jahrhunderts*. Leipzig, 1882, Alphons Dürr.

LARISCH, RUDOLF VON. *Beispiele künstlerischer Schrift aus vergangenen Jahrhunderten*. Wien, 1910, Staatsdruckerei.

LEAF, REUBEN. *Hebrew Alphabets*. New York, 1950.

LEHMANN-HAUPT, HELLMUT. *Calligrapher's paradise*. New York, 1942, A.D. Feb.-Mar.
———. *Initials from French Incunabula*. New York, 1948, Aldus.

LÖFFLER, KARL. *Romantische Zierbuchstaben und ihre Vorläufer*. Stuttgart, 1927, Hugo Matthaes.

MASON, WILLIAM ALBERT. *A history of the art of writing*. New York, 1920, MacMillan Co.

MASSEY, W. *The Origin and Progress of Letters*. London, 1763, J. Johnson.

MERKEN, JOHANN. *Liber artificiosus alphabeti majoris*. Mühlheim 1782–1785, J. C. Eyrich.

MOÉ, ÉMILE-A. VAN. *The decorated Letter*. Paris, 1950, Édition du Chêne.

MONUMENTA PALAEGRAPHICA. *Denkmäler der Schreibkunst des Mittelalters*. München, 1902–1917, F. Bruckmann.

MOORHOUSE, A. C. *Writing and the Alphabet*. London, 1946, Cobbett Press.

MÜLLER, DAVID HEINRICH and SCHLOSSER, JULIUS VON. *Die Haggadah von Sarajevo*. Wien, 1898, A. Hölder.

MUNCH, GOTTLIEB S. *Ordnung der Schrift*. Dresden, 1744.

MUNSCH, RENÉ H. *L'écriture et son dessin*. Paris, 1948, Eyrolles.

NEFF, CASPAR. *Thesaurarium artis scriptoriae*. Köln, 1549, Kaspar Vopelius.

*NESBITT, ALEXANDER. *Lettering, the History and Technique of Lettering as Design*. New York, 1950, Prentice-Hall.

NIEDLING, A. *Bücher-Ornamentik in Miniaturen, Initialen und Alphabeten im IX. bis XVIII. Jahrhundert*. Weimar, 1895, B. F. Voigt.

OGG, OSCAR. *The 26 Letters*. New York, 1948, Crowell.

PASERO, CARLO. *Libri di calligrafia*. Firenze, 1933, Bibliofilia.

PERICCIOLI. *Il terzo libro della cancellaresche corsive*. Siena, 1619.

PETZENDORFER, L. *Schriften Atlas*. Stuttgart, 1889, J. Hoffmann.

PISANI, GIOBATTISTA. *Tratteggiato da Penna*. Genova, 1640.

POLLARD, ALFRED W. *Some pictorial and heraldic initials*. London, 1897, Bibliographica.

POLYGRAPHIA CURIOSA. *The Book of Initial Letters and Ancient Alphabets for ornamental purposes*. London, 1844.

PREISLER, JOHANN DANIEL. *Orthographia*. Nürenberg, 1700, Johann Christoph Weigl.

SCHULZ, PHILIPP WALTER. *Die persisch-islamitische Miniaturmalerei*. Leipzig, 1914, K. W. Hiersemann.

*SCHWANDNER, JOHANN GEORG. *Dissertatio de Calligraphiae Nomenclatione Cultu, Praestantia, Utilitate.* Wien, 1756, Johann Leopold Kaliwoda.

SEDDON, JOHN. *The Pen-mans Paradis both Pleasant and Profitable.* London, 1695, Wm. Court.

SHAW, HENRY. *Alphabets, Numerals and Devices of the Middle Ages.* London, 1845.

———. *Hand Book of Mediaeval Alphabets and Devices.* London, 1856, Henry George Bohn.

SILVESTRE, JOSEPH BALTHAZAR. *Alphabet Album.* Paris, 1843–1844.

———. *Paléographie Universelle.* Paris, 1839–1841, Firmin Didot Fréres.

SMITH, WILLIAM ANDERSON. *According to Cocker.* London, 1887, A. Gardner.

STANDARD, PAUL. *Calligraphy's Flowering, Decay and Restauration.* Chicago, 1947, Soc. of Typographic Arts.

STRANGE, EDWARD FAIRBROTHER. *Alphabets.* London, 1895, G. Bell & Sons.

———. *The early English Writing Masters.* London, 1897, Bibliographica.

———. *The writing books of the 16th century.* London, 1896, Bibliographical Soc. Trans.

STRICK, MARIA. *Tooneel der loflijcke Schrijfpen.* Delft, 1607.

TAGLIENTE, GIOVANNI ANTONIO. *La vera arte dello eccellento scrivere.* Venezia, 1524, Stephano da Sabio.

THOMPSON, SIR EDWARD MAUNDE. *Calligraphy in the Middle Ages.* London, 1897, Bibliographica.

TSCHICHOLD, JAN. *Geschichte der Schrift in Bildern.* Basel, 1941, Holbein Verlag.

———. *Schatzkammer der Schreibkunst.* Basel, 1945, Birkhäuser.

VELDE, JAN VAN DEN. *Spieghel der Schrijfkonste.* Rotterdam, 1605.

VENTURA DA SILVA, JOAQUIM JOSÉ. *Regas Methodicas para se aprendera escrever.* Lisboa, 1803.

VESPASIANO DE FERRARE, AMPHIAREO. *Opera nellaquale si insegna a scrivere.* Venezia, 1554.

VICENTINO, LUDOVICO. *Regolo da imparare scrivere.* Venezia, 1533, Nicolo Zoppino.

WEALE, JOHN. *Monograms, old architectural ornaments, sacred illustrations, borders and alphabets.* London, 1852, Standidge & Co.

WEISE, OSKAR. *Schrift und Buchwesen in alter und neuer Zeit.* Leipzig, 1903, B. G. Teubner.

WILLIAMS, HENRY SMITH. *Manuscripts, inscriptions and muniments Oriental, comprehending the History of the Art of writing.* London, 1902, Merrill & Baker.

YANG YU-HSUN. *La Calligraphie Chinoise depuis les Han.* Paris, 1935, Paul Geuther.

YCIAR, JUAN DE. *Arte subtilissima por la qual se esseña a escrivir perfectamente.* Zaragoza, 1550.

ORNAMENTS AND PATTERN BOOKS

BANGE, ERNST FRIEDRICH. *Peter Flötner.* Leipzig, 1926, Meister der Graphik No. 14.

BAUD-BOVY, DANIEL. *Schweizer Bauerkunst.* Zürich, 1926, Orell Füssli.

BERLINER, RUDOLF. *Ornamentale Vorlageblätter des 15. bis 18. Jahrhunderts.* Leipzig, 1925, Klinkhardt & Biermann.

BOSSERT, HELMUTH THEODOR. *Ornament in applied art.* New York, 1924, E. Weyhe.

BRISVILLE, HUGUES. *Diverses pieces de Serruriers, engraved by Jean Berain.* Paris, 1663, N. Longlois.

COLUMNA, FRANCISCO. *Hypnerotomachia Poliphili.* Venezia, 1499, Aldus Manutius.

CRANACH THE ELDER, LUCAS. *Dye zaigung des hochlobwirdigen hailigthums der Stifft kirchen aller hailigen.* Wittenburg, 1509.

CUNDALL, JOSEPH. *On ornamented art, applied to ancient and modern bookbinding.* London, 1848, Society of Arts.

DOLMETSCH, HEINRICH. *Ornamental Treasures.* Stuttgart, 1912, J. Hoffmann.

———. *Der Ornamentenschatz.* Stuttgart, 1887, J. Hoffmann.

FLÖTNER, PETER. *Maureskenbuch.* Zürich, 1546, Rudolph Wyssenbach.

FOILLET, IAQUES. *Nouveaux pourtraicts de Point coupé.* Montbeliard, 1598.

FRANCO, GIACOMO. *Nuova inventione de diverse mostre.* Venezia, 1596.

GLAZIER, RICHARD. *The Manual of historic Ornament.* London, 1899, B. T. Batsford.

GRANLUND, STEN and JESSEN, JARNO. *Peasant art in Sweden, Lapland and Iceland.* London, 1910, The Studio.

GRUNER, LUDWIG (LEWIS). *Die Dekorative Kunst.* Dresden, 1881, Bleyl & Kaemmerer.

———. *Specimens of Ornamental Art.* London, 1850, T. M'Lean.

HABERLAND, M. *Peasant Art in Austria and Hungary.* London, 1911, The Studio.

HAMLIN, ALFRED DWIGHT FOSTER. *History of Ornament.* New York, 1916, Century.

HIRTH, GEORG. *Formenschatz.* München-Leipzig.

———. *Kulturgeschichtliches Bilderbuch.* München-Leipzig.

JESSEN, PETER. *Meister des Ornamentstiches.* Berlin, 1923, Verlag für Kunstwissenschaften.

———. *Der Ornamentstich.* Berlin, 1920, Verlag für Kunstwissenschaften.

JONES, OWEN. *Grammar of Ornaments.* London, 1856, Day & Son.

LICHTWARCK, ALFRED. *Der Ornamentstich der Deutschen Frührenaissance.* Berlin, 1888, Weidemannsche Buchhandlung.

LOTZ, ARTHUR. *Bibliographie der Modelbücher.* Leipzig, 1933, K. W. Hiersemann.

MAROT, DANIEL. *Das Ornamentwerk des. . . .* Berlin, 1892, Ernst Wasmuth.

*MEYER, FRANZ SALES. *Handbuch der Ornamentik.* Leipzig, 1890, E. A. Seemann.

OPRESCU, G. *Peasant Art in Rumania.* London, 1929, The Studio.

OSTAUS, GIOVANNI. *La vera perfettione del disegno di varie sorti per punti i Ricami.* Venezia, 1567.

PAGAN, MATTHEO. *Giardinetto novo di punti tagliati.* Venezia, 1543.

PAGANINO, ALESSANDRO P. *Il burato libro de recami.* Venezia, 1518.

PELLEGRIN, FRANCESQUE. *Lafleur de la science de Pourtraicture.* Paris, 1530.

PUGIN, AUGUSTUS WELBY NORTHMORE. *A Glossary of Ecclesiastical Ornament.* London, 1844, Bernard Quaritch.

QUENTEL, PETER. *Eyn newe kunstlich moetdelboeck.* Cöllen, 1532.

RACINET, ALBERT CHARLES AUGUSTE. *L'Ornement polychrome.* Paris, 1885, Firmin Didot & Cie.

REYNARD, OVIDE. *Ornaments des Anciens Maîtres des XVe, XVIe, XVIIe et XVIII Siècles.* Paris. 1844, A. Lèvy.

RICCI, ELISA. *Antiche trine Italiane raccolte e ordinate.* Bergamo, 1908, Instituto Italiano d'Arti Grafiche.

ROETTINGER, HEINRICH. *Peter Flötners Holzschnitte.* Strassburg, 1916, J. H. E. Heitz.

SHAW, HENRY. *The Decorative Arts, Ecclesiastical and Civil, of the Middle Ages.* London, 1851, William Pickering.

———. *The Encyclopedia of Ornament.* London, 1842, William Pickering.

SIBMACHER, HANS. *Schön Neues Modelbuch von allerley lustigen Mödeln.* Nürnberg, 1597, Balthaser Xaimoyen.

*SPELTZ, ALEXANDER. *Styles of Ornament.* New York, 1908.

STAUD, JOHN JOSEPH. *Pennsylvania Folk-Art.* Allentown, Pa., 1948, Schlechter's.

STRANGE, EDWARD FAIRBROTHER. *Early pattern-books of lace, embroidery and needlework.* London, 1902, Bibliographical Society Trans. No. 7.

STUDIO, THE. *Peasant Art in Italy.* London, 1913.

———. *Peasant Art in Russia.* London.

TERRY, GARNET. *Commeditor, A Book of New and Allegorical Devices.* London, 1795, Bowles & Carner.

UBISCH, E. *Über Spitzenbücher und Spitzen.* Berlin, 1893, Repertorium für Kunstwissenschaften.

VAVASORE, GIOVANNI ANDREA. *Essemplario di lavori.* Venezia, 1532.

VINCIOLO, FEDERIC DE. *Les singuliers et nouveaux pourtraicts, pour toutes sortes d'ouvrages de Lingeries.* Paris, 1606, Jean le Clerc.

WARD, JAMES. *Historic Ornament.* London, 1897, Chapman & Hall.

ZAHN, W. *Ornamente aller Klassischen Kunst-Epochen.* Berlin, 1849.

ZOPPINO, NICOLO. *Essemplario di lavori.* Venezia, 1529.

SILHOUETTES AND SHADOW PUPPETS

BEUNINGEN VAN HELSDINGEN, R. VAN. *The Javanese Theatre.* Singapore, 1913, Royal Asiatic Society Straits Branch Journal No. 65.

BOEHN, MAX VON. *Miniaturen und Silhouetten.* München, 1919, F. Bruckmann.

BUSS, GEORG. *Aus der Blütezeit der Silhouette.* Leipzig, 1913, Xenien.

COKE, DESMOND. *The art of silhouette.* London, 1913, Martin Secker.

DELACHAUX, THEODCR. *Un artiste paysan du Pays d'Enhaut, Jean Jacob Hauswirth.* Basel, 1916, Schweizer Archiv für Volkskunde.

GRIAULE, MARCEL. *Silhouettes et graffiti abyssins.* Paris, 1933, Larose.

GUDENRATH, EDUARD. *Exotische Schattenspiele und die Belebungsversuche im Abendland.* 1927, Das Theater, Oktober.

HAWLEY, W. N. *Chinese Folk Design.* Hollywood, 1949.

HEGE, WALTER. *Griechische Schattenspiele.* Berlin, 1930, Atlantis, September.

HOEVER, OTTO. *Javanische Schattenspiele.* Leipzig, 1923, Wilhelm Goldmann.

JACKSON-NEVILLE, EMILY. *History of Silhouettes.* London, 1911, The Connoisseur.

JACOB, GEORG. *Einführung in die altchinesischen Schattenspiele.* Stuttgart, 1935, W. Kohlhammer.

————. *Geschichte des Schattentheaters im Morgen- und Abendland.* Hannover, 1935, Heinz Lafaire.

————. *Die Herkunft der Silhouetten-Kunst aus Persien.* Berlin, 1917, Mayer & Müller.

————. *Schattenschnitte aus Nordchina.* Hannover, 1923, Heinz Lafaire.

———— and JENSEN, HANS. *Das Chinesische Schattentheater.* Stuttgart, 1933, W. Kohlhammer.

————. *Das Indische Schattentheater.* Stuttgart, 1931, W. Kohlhammer.

KAHLE, PAUL. *Islamitische Schattenspielfiguren aus Egypten.* Strassburg, 1910–11, Der Islam.

————. *Der Leuchtturm von Alexandria.* Stuttgart, 1930, W. Kohlhammer.

KNAPP, MARTIN. *Deutsche Schatten- und Scherenbilder aus drei Jahrhunderten.* Dachau, Der Gelbe Verlag.

KUNST, J. *Een en ander over de Javaansche Wajang.* Amsterdam, 1940, Koloniaal Instituut Mededeeling No. 53.

MÄRTEN, LU. *Schattenrisse von einem anonymen Wiener Meister des 18. Jahrhunderts.* Wien, 1913, E. Beyerl's Nachflg.

MÉGROZ, RODOLPHE LOUIS. *Profile art through the ages.* London, 1948, The Art Trade Press.

MELCHERS, BERND. *Chinesische Scherenschnitte.* München, 1921, H. Bruckmann.

MUELLER, F. W. K. *Nang, Siamesische Schattenspiele.* Leiden, 1894, Internationales Archiv für Ethnographie.

NANYO KYOKAI. *Wajang, Javanese puppet shadow picture shows.* Tokyo, 1941, South Sea Association Bulletin, February.

PAZAUREK, GUSTAV E. *Schwarzkunst in Schwaben.* 1909, Westermanns Monatshefte, Januar.

PHILLIPS, HENRY A. *China's vanishing shadow shows.* New York, 1934, Asia, July.

SCHÜLLER, SEPP. *Das javanische Wajang-Schattenspiel.* Zürich, 1935, Atlantis, Februar.

SEEMANN, ARTHUR. *Japanische Färbeschablonen.* Leipzig, 1899.

SERRURIER, LINDOR. *De Wajang poerwa, eene ethnologische Studie.* Leiden, 1896, E. J. Brill.

SPAMER, ADOLF. *Das kleine Andachtsbild vom 14 bis zum 20. Jahrhundert.* München, 1930, F. Bruckmann.

STERLING, ADELINE. *The shadowplay in Siam.* Weltevreden, 1932, Inter Ocean.

WAJANG PURWA. *Das Javanische Schattenspiel.* Braunschweig, 1898, Globus.

WIMSATT, GENEVIEVE. *Chinese shadow shows.* Cambridge, Mass., 1936, Harvard University Press.

YUYNBOLL, H. H. *Javanische Schattenspiele.* Leiden, 1900, Internationales Archiv für Ethnographie.

HERALDIC ORNAMENTS AND MAP CARTOUCHES

ALMAGIA, R. *Monumenta Italiae Cartographica.* Firenze, 1929, Instituto Geografico Militare.

AMMAN, JOST. *Wapen und Stambuch.* Frankfurt a.M., 1579–1589, Sigmund Feyerabend.

BAUER, KONRAD F. *Das Bürgerwappen.* Frankfurt a.M., 1935, Hauserpresse.

————. *Der Greif.* Frankfurt a.M., 1939, Bauersche Giesserei.

BERCHEM, EGON VON. *Die Wappenbücher des Deutschen Mittelalters.* Basel, 1928, Emil Birkhäuser.

BOUTELL, CHARLES. *English Heraldry.* London, 1867, Reeves & Turner.

BROWN, LLOYD A. *The Story of Maps.* Boston, 1950, Little, Brown & Co.

CHUBB, T. *The Printed Maps in the Atlases of Great Britain and Ireland.* London, 1927, Homeland Association.

COLE, HERBERT. *Heraldry and Floral Forms as used in Decoration.* London, 1922, J. M. Dent & Sons.

COPINGER, WALTER ARTHUR. *Heraldry simplified.* Manchester, 1910, University Press.

DAVENPORT, CYRIL. *English Heraldic Book Stamps.* London, 1909, Archibald Constable & Co.

FITE, EMERSON DAVID and FREEMAN, ARCHIBALD. *A Book of Old Maps Delineating American History.* Cambridge, Mass., 1926, Harvard University Press.

FLETCHER, W. Y. *English Armorial Book Stamps and their owners.* London, 1897, Bibliographica.

FORDHAM, SIR HERBERT GEORGE. *Maps, their History, Characteristics and Uses.* Cambridge, 1921, University Press.

Fox-Davies, Arthur Charles. *Complete Guide to Heraldry*. London, 1925, T. C. & E. C. Jack.
———. *Fairbairn's Book of Crests*. Edinburgh, 1892, T. C. & F. C. Jack.

Galbreath, Donald Lindsay. *A treatise on ecclesiastical Heraldry*. Cambridge, 1930, W. Heffer & Sons.
———. *Handbüchlein der Heraldik*. Lausanne, 1948, Spes-Verlag.
Grant, Francis J. *The Manual of Heraldry*. Edinburgh, 1948, John Grant.

Hope, Sir William Henry St. John. *Heraldry for Craftsmen and Designers*. London, 1913, J. Hogg.
Humphreys, Arthur Lee. *Old Decorative Maps and Charts*. London, 1926, H. & T. Smith.

Jomard, Edme Francois. *Les Monuments de la Geographie*. Paris, 1842–1862.

Lehmann, Edgar. *Alte Deutsche Landkarten*. Leipzig, 1935, Bibliographisches Institut.
L'Isle, Guillaume de. *La France*. Paris, 1703.
Lynam, Edward. *British Maps and Mapmakers*. London, 1944, W. Collins.
Lynch-Robinson, Sir Christopher. *Intelligible Heraldry*. London, 1949, McDonald.

Magny, Ludovic Viscomte de. *Nobiliaire Universel*. Paris, 1854–1880, Institut Héraldique.
Merian, Matheus. *Topographia Galliae*. Basel, 1555, Caspar Merian.
Münster, Sebastian. *Cosmographey, oder beschreibung aller Länder, herrschafften und fürnembsten Stetten des gantzen Erdbodens*. Basel, 1578, Henric Petri.

Nordenskiöld, Adolf Erick. *Facsimile-Atlas to the early History of cartography*. Stockholm, 1889.

Ortelius, Abraham. *Theatrum orbis terrarum*. Antwerpen, 1570–1584.
Ortroy, F. van. *Remarkable Maps of the XV., XVI., and XVII. century*. Amsterdam, 1894–1897, F. Muller.

Paris. *Atlas des anciens plans de Paris*. Paris, 1880, Department de Seine.
Parker, John H. and James. *The Annals of England*. Oxford, 1855–1857.

Rothery, Guy Cadogan. *The A.B.C. of Heraldry*. Philadelphia, 1915, G. W. Jacobs & Co.

Speed, John. *The Theatre of the Empire of Great-Britaine*. London, 1612.
Ströhl, Hugo Gerard. *Heraldischer Atlas*. Stuttgart, 1899, Julius Hoffmann.
Stückelberg, Ernst Alfred. *Das Wappen in Kunst und Gewerbe*. Zürich, 1901.

Tooley, R. V. *Maps and Mapmakers*. London-New York, 1949, B. T. Batsford.

Warnecke, Friedrich. *Heraldische Kunstblätter*. Görlitz, 1877–1891.
———. *Heraldisches Handbuch für Freunde der Wappenkunst*. Frankfurt a.M., 1893, Heinrich Keller.
Weller, Ernst. *Roland—Archiv für Stamm- und Wappenkunde*. Kahla i.Th., 1902–1921, Gebr. Vogt Papiermühle.
Wieder, Frederik Caspar. *Monumenta cartographica*. Den Haag, 1925–1934, Martinus Nijhoff.
Wyon, Alfred Benjamin. *The great Seals of England*. London, 1887, Chiswick Press.

Zieber, Eugene. *Heraldry in America*. Philadelphia, 1895, Bailey, Banks & Biddle.